AF505357

Jutta Vinzent

OVERcoming DICTatorships

Contemporary
East and West European
Visual Inquiries

KERBER ART

OVERcoming DICTatorships

Contemporary
East and West European
Visual Inquiries

Zbyněk **Benýšek**
Zbigniew **Czop**
Mirela **Dauceanu**
Ulf **Göpfert**
Harald **Hauswald**
Silvestro **Lodi**
Vlad **Nancă**
Sándor **Pinczehelyi**
Michele **Zaggia**
Aleksander **Zyśko**

Over Dict

Appendices

Introduction

Introduction

Overcoming Dictatorships explores art produced in response to the collapse of authoritarian political systems, particularly those of the Soviet bloc in 1989, which, as will be argued, caused ideological dislocations and relocations. The book's subtitle could have also included a reference to Post-Communism or Post-Socialism,[1] but the issues raised cover slightly different territories than such references would indicate, not least because it also considers art produced in the so-called 'West' in addition to that from East European countries, both terms which will be contested in this book. Laura Hoptman and Tomáš Pospiszyl have proposed that East Europe does not designate a geographically precise locoation.[2] Describing, if at all, geopolitical regions whose politico-economic *histories* differ from those of West Europe, but whose borders are not clearly defined, both concepts, however, are firmly established in academia through institutions and publications and therefore led to the subtitling of this book as *Contemporary East and West European Visual Inquiries*.[3]

A case in point will be works produced by ten artists who have been selected by 'Overcoming Dictatorships', a project generously funded by the European Union (EU) from 2006 to 2009.[4] Its aim has been to create a dialogue between writers and artists on experiences of the change from dictatorships to democracies and also to improve communication between East and West Europe, and thus challenging such conventional conceptions in a Europe which is in need of being newly conceptualized after the end of the Soviet bloc.[5]

Interest in the contemporary art produced in the countries involved, particularly the former Soviet satellite states, is increasing. Many exhibitions and publications, however, focus on one country only, with a few exceptions. The closest to the undertaking here is *Against. Within*, an anthology which publishes the results of another project funded under the same scheme.[6] Although focusing on a slightly different topic, that of the forms of critique before and after the collapse of Communism, its participants came from formerly Eastern and West European countries.[7] In this respect, it differs from all the other publications mentioned in the following, which concentrated only on East Europe or countries new to the EU.

A hermaphrodite position is taken by *East Art Map*, a massive anthology compared with the former and the present one (built on a decade-long project), published by Central Saint Martin's College of Art and Design in London in 2006:[8] It only explores artists from the East, but includes both locally renowned ones and those with an international background, who exchanged their roots by moving to the West (such as Ilya Kabakov and Maria Abramović). Hence it contributes to bridging the East with the West in its own way, although different from the present undertaking, which looks at artists still connected with their national and cultural origins.

Among those works which considers solely the Eastern part of Europe is the exhibition *B-Zone. Becoming Europe and Beyond*, which grew out of a research project on transitory geographies and was held at the KE Institute for Contemporary Art in Berlin in 2005 and 2006 and at the Fundació Tàpies in Barcelona in 2007.[9] While it concentrated on different countries (i.e. Southeast Europe, the Balkans, Greece, Turkey and the Caucasus) and involved a different kind of visual output,[10] it followed similar working practices and aims as 'Overcoming Dictatorships', namely to bring 'the reflection process closer to the fieldwork and in direct contact with art and intellectual circuits', centring on 'problems of representation, visuality, and unburied histories.'[11]

A further exhibition related to this topic is *Arrivals – Art from the New Europe* held at the Modern Museum in Oxford in 2005, the result of a two-year collaboration between Modern Art Oxford and Turner Contemporary, which introduces the work of artists from the expanded EU.[12] The publication covers the ten 'Arrivals' countries to the EU in 2004 – Poland, Slovenia, Lithuania, Latvia, Czech Republic, Cyprus, Slovakia, Estonia, Hungary and Malta – and includes images of the artists' works, their installation displays in the exhibitions and behind-the-scene photographs. The exhibition attempts to overcome its intrinsically Westernized title *Arrivals* (as if these countries have not existed in Europe before) through essays by gallery directors, curators, critics and art historians from across the EU.[13]

While the selection of the countries for *Arrivals* was based on the relationship to the EU, those for the exhibition *Crossing Frontiers* held in the Kunstforum Ostdeutsche Galerie in Regensburg in 2006 and the Ludwig Museum of Contemporary Art in Budapest in the following year primarily focused on previously Communist countries and East European identities,[14] as did *After the Wall*, shown at the Moderna Museet, Stockholm in 1999 and at the Ludwig Museum of Contemporary Art in Budapest in 2000. Initially a research project which resulted in an exhibition, a publication and a symposium,[15] the latter was a much larger venture dedicated to art and culture of the decade 1989-99 in post-Communist Europe, revealing, according to David Elliott, the director of the Moderna Museet in Stockholm and co-editor of the exhibition catalogue, 'that this is a state of being which can reflect many different realities. In the space of ten years the map of Europe has been redrawn and along with it many individuals' sense of identity and belonging.'[16] The catalogue revolves around the themes of art as a kind of 'social sculpture', the impact of history on identity definitions, personal and artistic subjectivity in governments in which the individual was formerly subordinated to the collective and the issues of gender constructions as different from Communist stereotypes, which 'claimed to give universal emancipation.'[17]

Different from *Overcoming Dictatorships* (and in this respect also from *Crossing Frontiers*), however, *After the Wall* interpreted art in a broader sense, including also music and performance from 22 countries, among them all those formerly Soviet satellite states involved in this project. Being shown

Fig. 1

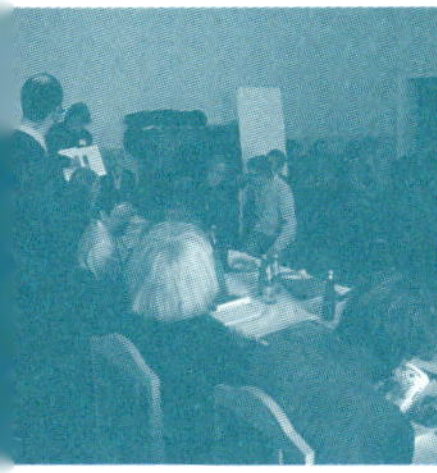

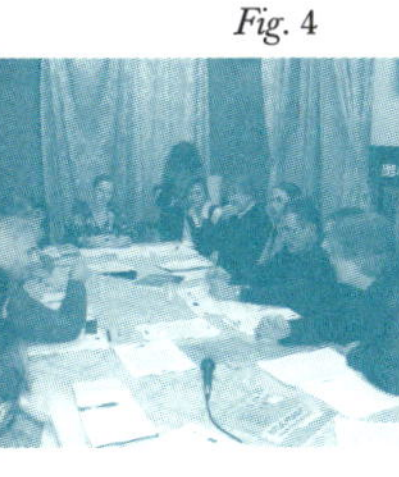

Fig. 2

Fig. 3

Fig. 4

Fig. 5

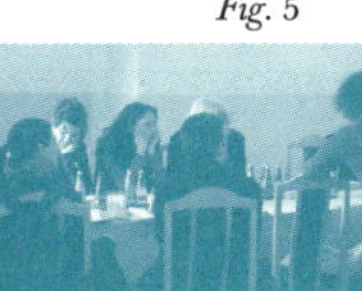

in 1999, it could only consider the 1990s, whereas *Overcoming Dictatorships* covers the years until the beginning of 2008, years in which particularly the EU's map has been redrawn again and again (Romania, for example, only joined on 1 January 2007). And although the themes in *After the Wall* also play a role in *Overcoming Dictatorships*, the latter project does not primarily look back to a state *after*, but understands itself as being part of ongoing reflective processes of 'overcoming.'

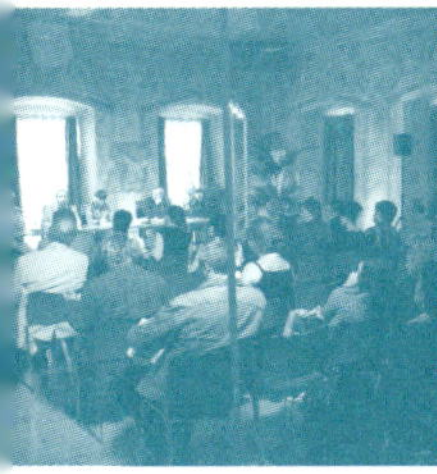

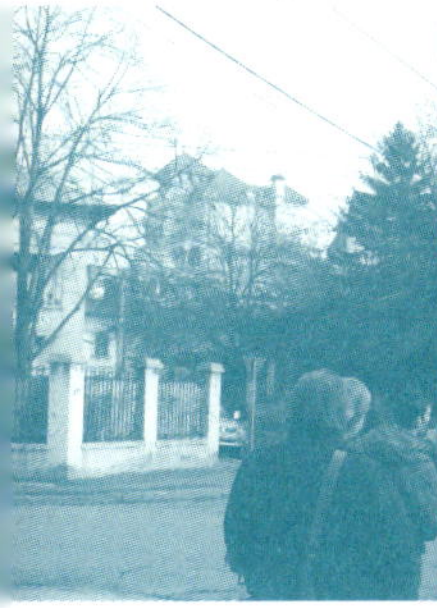

The artists (visual artists and writers) themselves together with guest speakers from the countries involved have been participating in, and their works hence have grown out of, the discussions held at the workshops which were organized as part of the project [*Figs.* 1 and 2].[18] These workshops offered the artists the opportunity to get in contact with each other, to visit each other in order to discover the living and working environments in their respective countries [*Fig.* 3], and to jointly reflect on and exchange experiences which they have made or undergone before and since 1989 [*Fig.* 4]. The meetings, which have been filmed, constitute primary material for the project and also for this book, which is thus informed methodologically by oral history.[19] The project culminates for the artists in a touring exhibition entitled *Overcoming Dictatorships*.[20] To continue the encounter and the reflection on the processes of ideological migration also between and beyond the seven workshops, the project used an interactive web log (http://overcomings.blogspot.com/).

In the round table discussion at the first workshop with the artists held in Poland from 30 March to 1 April 2007 [*Fig.* 5], the artists questioned the title of the project; they emphasized the significance of reflecting the past, describing various forms of 'overcoming' as mourning for and remembering the past. They also mentioned the generational gap: the project involved artists who had lived under the Communist regime, such as Sándor Pinczehelyi from Pécs (Hungary), born in 1946, but also those who had been children then, including Vlad Nancă from Bucharest (Romania), born in 1979. The artists also addressed the present and drew attention to newly encountered dictatorships as regards religions, economies, art media, networks and globalization.[21]

How do artists who experienced the challenging changes relate to the year 1989 and the then forced or enabled ideological migration caused by collective political-economic upheavals respond visually to their own specific 'locations'? Applying concepts which have been developed for and amply applied to physical migration,[22] the works in question will be explored as signifiers of ideological dislocations and relocations experienced in terms of both the past (through processes of mourning and remembering and attempts at overcoming) and the present (critical approach to the ideology of the Western art market, the new political government and Europe), thus neglecting a mainly object-oriented formalist and aesthetic analysis as well as psychoanalytical methodologies and putting issues related to Postcolonialism to the fore. It also only touches on gender issues, because, as highlighted above, this valuable topic deserves treatment in its own right.[23] The variety of the individual artist's responses on the one hand and the relatively small number of art works explored on the other hand defy any attempt to subsume their individualities into a 'grande narrative' or as the start of a new 'democratic' history of longue durée, as if they simply could be incorporated into old, existing Western categories as markers of the latter's superiority and longevity. On the contrary, the works discussed revolt against new communal enclaves and rather represent attempts of individuals to overcome given collective identity formations and to question both the political past, the EU and Western democracies.

[1] For the use of Socialism in reference to Communism, see Bojana Pejić, 'The dialectics of normality', Bojana Pejić and David Elliott (eds.), *After the Wall. Art and Culture in Post-Communist Europe*, exh. cat., Stockholm, Moderna Museet, 1999 and Budapest, Ludwig-Museum of Contemporary Art, 2000, 016-028, 016. Susan Buck-Morss, 'Theorizing Today: The Post-Soviet Condition', *Log*, winter issue, 2008, 23-31, 23 expresses her tiredness of the 'posts': 'We are suffering from a kind of postpartum depression,' fearing a new start.

[2] See Laura Hoptman and Tomáš Pospiszyl, 'Introduction', Laura Hoptman and Tomáš Pospiszyl (eds.), *Primary Documents. A Sourcebook for Eastern and Central European Art since the 1950s*, Cambridge/Mass., 2002, 9-11, 9.

[3] See, for example, the titles of the following series: *East European Politics and Societies; Tübinger Mittel- und Osteuropastudien – Politik, Gesellschaft, Kultur* and *Schriften der Deutschen Gesellschaft für Osteuropakunde*. The following are examples of institutionalization: the leading think tank in Hungary, the Teleki László Intézet (the Teleki Institute), which is subtitled as Centre for East European Studies (Közép-Európai Tanulmányok Központja); the Russian and East European Institute at Indiana University, Bloomington (USA), which also has a Center for West European Studies, and the School of Slavonic, Central and East European Studies at the University of Glasgow (UK). See also the British Library 'Slavonic and East European Collections' (British Library, London, UK). The West is probably more established as a concept than in institutional names and explored, for example, by James Carrier (ed.), *Occidentalism. Images of the West*, Oxford, 1995 and Ute Dietrich and Martina Winkler (eds.), *Okzidentbilder. Konstruktionen und Wahrnehmungen*, Leipzig, 2000. The West has received wide criticism for excluding particularly the ethnically others (see, for example, James Elkins, *Stories of Art*, New York and London, 2002).

[4] Each of the artists has contributed a text published under 'In the Artists' Voices.'

[5] In accordance with the guidelines of the Culture 2000 Scheme, institutions in seven countries have been involved: project management and main applicant has been Prof. Dr. Dr. Gerhard Besier, chair for European Studies at the Technische Universität Dresden in Germany, Prof. Dr. Ehrhard Cziomer from Krakowska Szkoła Wyższa im. Andrzeja Frycza Modrzewskiego in Kraków (Poland), Dr. Marius Oprea, Director of the Institute for the Investigation of Communist Crimes in Romania in Bucharest, Romania, Doc. PhDr. Kristina Kaiserová CSc. from the University of Jan Evangelista Purkyně in Ústí nad Labem, Czech Republic, Katalin Gádoros for Prof. Dr. István Rév from the Open Society Archives (OSA) at the University of Budapest, Hungary, Prof. Dr. Gustavo Corni from the University of Trent, Italy, and Dr. Dr. Jutta Vinzent from, the Department of History of Art, University of Birmingham, UK. While members of five post-Communist countries could reflect on the more current opening of the Iron Curtain, Italy and also Germany have been able to look at the topic from the perspective of a so called Second Generation. Britain has been involved because, as we argued in the application form, albeit not having faced dictator-ships, it established authoritarian systems known as colonies. The project also created a website (http://lehrstuhl-europastudien.eu/eu/). The partners from these seven countries suggested artists and writers who were then invited to take part in the workshops. We decided not to include artists from Britain, since we felt that a comparison between artists producing works which relate to Post-colonialism and those involved here is a subject in its own right.

The project has been mentioned by Sarah James, 'Behind a Theoretical *Iron Curtain*', *Art Monthly*, June 2008, 7-10, 10, as one of those which have 'started to turn to those neglected histories of Eastern European avant-garde and modernist art practices.'

[6] See Ilina Koralova (ed.), *Against. Within*, Graz, 2006.

[7] See Ilina Koralova, 'Introduction', Ilina Koralova (ed.), *Against. Within*, 7-9, 7. The instutions involved were the Galerie für Zeitgenössische Kunst Leipzig (Germany), the Department of Art and Design at the J. E. Purkyně University in Ústí nad Labem (Czech Republic), the Forum Stadtpark Graz (Austria), Van Abbe Museum in Eindhoven (Netherlands), the Škuc Gallery in Ljubljana (Slovenia) and the Institute for Contemporary Art in Dunaújváros (Hungary).

[8] Irwin (ed.), *East Art Map. Contemporary Art and Eastern Europe*, London, 2006.

[9] Anselm Franke (ed.), *B-Zone. Becoming Europe and Beyond*, Berlin and Barcelona, 2006. The title's 'B' refers to 'becoming' and designates a 'zoned and fragmented area' (see Anselm Franke, 'Introduction', *ibid.*, 6-15, 6).

10   The illustrations in *B-Zone's* catalogue are more of a documentary nature, including topographic photographs, maps
and depictions of a moment in people's daily life as
well as travel diaries, while 'Overcoming Dictatorships' is
more concerned with the artists' oral and visual inquiries
into the theme of the project.

11   See Ursula Biemann, 'Preface', Anselm Franke (ed.),
B-Zone, 4f., 4. Similar working practices refer to
the workshops held in locations relevant to the project.

12   Suzanne Cotter, Andrew Nairne and Victoria Pomery (eds.),
Arrivals>Art from the New Europe, exh. cat., Oxford, Modern
Art Oxford and Turner Contemporary, 2007.

13   See Karel Císa , 'Toward "Minor" Art' in the very same
exhibition catalogue of Suzanne Cotter, Andrew Nairne
and Victoria Pomery (eds.), *Arrivals,* 106f., 106, who
criticizes the Czech reception of the country's accession to
the EU which was seen as an enactment of the 'return to
Europe': 'Any "return to Europe" assumes that the Soviet
Bloc countries were outside Europe, identified as the
geopolitical West.' A further example for viewing the
countries from the former Soviet bloc in a similar way is
the title of a book by Michael Palin, *New Europe,* London,
2007, which is a diary written alongside his popular
documentary series on BBC television in 2007 and 2008.

14   See Kunstforum Ostdeutsche Galerie Regensburg (ed.),
Crossing Frontiers. Határátl Épések. Grenzgänger, exh. cat.,
Regensburg, Kunstforum Ostdeutsche Galerie, 2006 and
Budapest, Museum of Contemporary Art/Ludwig
Museum, 2007.

15   See David Elliott, 'Introduction', Bojana Pejić and David
Elliott (eds.), *After the Wall,* 011.

16   *Ibid.,* 011.

17   *Ibid.*

18   Except for the first, discussions during the workshops
were filmed by Barbara Lubich (Dresden/Trent).
Particularly relevant are the second, third and fourth
workshops also cited in the bibliography.

19   Further material includes artists' questionnaires
(see bibliography) and portraits of artists also filmed by
Barbara Lubich.

20   The exhibition will be shown at the University of
Birmingham (Aston Webb Building), UK, from 9 Oct. to
9 Nov. 2008 and then travel to Kraków (Poland), where it
will be shown at the KSW from 17 Nov. to 7 Dec. 2008,
then Bucharest (Romania) from 13 Dec. 2008 to 4 Jan. 2009,
the Open Society Archives Gallery, Budapest (Hungary)
from 12 to 25 Jan., the Municipal Gallery at Torre Mirana
in Trent (Italy) from 31 Jan. to 22 Feb. 2009, Gallery
Castle Děčin in Ústí nad Labem (Czech Republic) from 28
Feb. to 21 March and then in the Town Hall in Dresden
(Germany) from 29 March to 26 April 2009. The exact
location of the exhibition in Bucharest was not confirmed
when this book went to print. 17 works will be shown
(partly newly produced, partly already existing works).
Illustrations of these works can be found under 'In the
Artists' Voices'. The way the project was set up meant the
artists had a major say about the inclusion of works in the
exhibition *Overcoming Dictatorships.* Therefore, the exhibition
is in some sense a work with participation character. The

term 'participation' has been hijacked from Claire Bishop,
Participation. Documents of Contemporary Art, London and
Cambridge, 2006. In her introduction, she defines
participation as referring to the social dimension of art,
which emphasizes 'collaboration and the collective
dimension of social experience.' For her, one of the first
people to elaborate theoretically the political status of
participation was Walter Benjamin (see *ibid.,* 11).

21   We found that the language in which to communicate best
during these workshops was English with some translations. The catalogue is also published in English since it
has become the *lingua franca* for contemporary art and also
serves as a mediator in art instead of being an essential
part of the medium as, for example, in literary writings,
although self-critically, the author is aware of the
'dictatorship' of language which Antonio de Nebrija calls
the 'perfect instrument of empire.' Cited after Roger
Conover, 'Against Dictionaries: The East As She Is Spoke
By the West', Irwin (ed.), *East Art Map,* 349-361, 349.

22   For example, Jutta Vinzent, *Identity and Image. Refugee Artists
from Nazi Germany in Britain, 1933-1945,* Kromsdorf/
Weimar, 2006.

23   Such a study could draw on Eva Kolinsky and Hildegard
Maria Nickel (eds.), *Reinventing Gender. Women in Eastern
Germany Since Unification,* London, 2003.

1 Processes of Overcoming Dictatorships

Notwithstanding initial criticisms, the term 'dictatorships' seems to be a common denominator that is more clearly shaped than 'overcoming' and with which those involved in the project have been able to identify. Conventionally, the term has been used to refer to political non-democratic regimes such as the autocratic governments in the first half of the twentieth century,[24] but also Caesarism and Bonapartism.[25] It also refers to regimes of the former Soviet bloc countries[26] as well as to a variety of undemocratic ways of using power, such as the authority of the viewer and curator in the arts.[27] The broader use of the term, of course, undermines the specific connotations that have historically developed. Norberto Bobbio argues that the term 'dictatorship' became widespread only after the First World War, 'both in the heated debate on the form of government established by the Bolsheviks and in the descriptions of fascist regimes, beginning with the Italian, which were employed by their opponents.'[28] Technically more correct, as Bobbio suggests, would be the term autocracy, as 'dictatorship' allows us to include not only violence and oppression under the veil of an institution as, for example, 'Roman dictatorship' with the exclusion of personal responsibility, but also the implication of positive aspects or a form of government modelled on it termed by Bobbio 'revolutionary dictatorship.'[29]

Despite its even less clear definition, those involved in the project explored the designation and interpretation of 'overcoming', subsequently addressed and scrutinized in a variety of the artists' works as outlined in the following.

It is probably characteristic of the younger generation, having experienced the regime only as children and in terms of financial hardship and rationed food, but not as an oppression or restriction of freedom, that Nancă has emphasized the positive aspects of Ceauşescu's Romania. His standpoint contradicts the official statement of Marius Oprea, the president of the Institute for the Investigation of Communist Crimes in Romania, who is one of the partners in the EU project: 'Many people are asking whether an outright condemnation of communism is still necessary, now that 16 years have passed since the Revolution of 1989. I say it is, and I rely on the fact that such a profoundly moral decision, meant to restore the Romanian society from its foundation, is necessary at any time.'[30]

In contrast, Nancă mourns changes for the socially worse, pointing to

Fig. 6

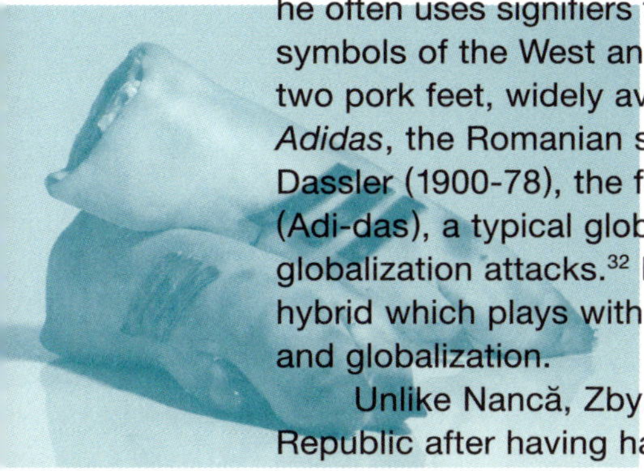

better neighbourly and personal relationships before 1989, better care for the environment and the voluntary engagement in social activities.[31] In his art, he often uses signifiers to remember the time before, playing with and blurring symbols of the West and East: In *Original Adidas* of 2003 [*Fig.*6], he takes two pork feet, widely available in Communist Romania, and entitles his work, *Adidas*, the Romanian slang for these. This is also the acronym for Adolf Dassler (1900-78), the founder of a (West) German sports show factory (Adi-das), a typical global brand that, like Nike, has been a target for anti-globalization attacks.[32] Nancă adds six Velcro stripes, thus creating a cultural hybrid which plays with notions of the local past and Western consumerism and globalization.

Fig. 7 see page 49

Unlike Nancă, Zbyněk Benýšek, who can live once again in the Czech Republic after having had to leave in 1982, openly criticizes the dictatorial past. In his surrealist painting *Saint Sebastian* of 1993 [*Fig.*7], he shows three people sitting on a futuristic computer-like machine, which, according to the artist, was needed in order to be able to cope with the numerous inquisitions into the undertakings of so many people in Communist Czechoslovakia.[33] Applying Christian iconography that conventionally depicts Saint Sebastian as tied to a post and attacked by arrows, the martyr stands for those who suffered under dictatorships. The surrealist style, which is also used by other painters in the Czech Republic (for example Jakub Hošek), can be seen as an allegory for the collapse of modern utopia, as suggested by Tomás Pospiszyl for Czech art of the 1990s in general.[34]

Zbigniew Czop, who lives and works in Kraków (Poland), has a different approach. He agrees that we cannot forget the past; people bear scars from that time, both physical and mental. He took part in the project with the aim in mind of informing people about these scars.[35] Along similar lines, Aleksander Zyśko from Wrocław (Poland) has produced *Sickle and Hammer*

Fig. 8 see page 81

[*Fig.*8], a sculpture he made shortly after the end of the Communist era in Poland in 1991. As a widespread Communist icon of the industrial proletariat and the peasantry, it was also used on the national flag of the USSR until its disintegration on 25 December 1991 and on several Communist Party flags. Hence the sickle and hammer not only symbolize the unity between industrial and agricultural workers, they also represent an ideology, whose realization has come to an end; indeed, they are broken into two pieces by Zyśko. Does the artist indicate the end of the Soviet hegemony and Communist power, the break-up of the link between industry and agriculture, or is he reminding us of a past that had already ceased to exist and can be only symbolically revoked?

Fig. 9 see page 80

His other work, *Cross in Cross* of 1990 [*Fig.*9], uses another power symbol. It hints at the influence of the Catholic Church both in Communist times, but also after 1989. The church's dominating role in promoting opposition views, its close relationship with the influential trade union Solidarity and its mediation between factions in the 1980s brought it enhanced political power in post-Communist Poland as well.[36] Gerhard Besier argues that the church saw its function not only to 're-Catholicize' the country, but also to act as a

catalyst for the re-Christianization of Europe.' In 'Poland almost nothing
works without the Catholic Church. The conservative wing still controls large
portions of life in society. Liberal forces within Catholicism that were
also active in the opposition, on the other hand, remained restricted to the
periphery.'[37]

Remembering after forgetting is the motto of Lutz Rathenow, who
published several books together with Harald Hauswald, notably *Gewendet,*
which continues in some ways their *Ost-Berlin* book.[38] While Rathenow as
the writer contributes memories, aphorisms and stories, Hauswald provides
black-and-white photographs, which have also been shown at a variety of
international galleries.[39] Hauswald's contribution to the EU project's exhibition,
Time Travels of 2008 [*Fig.*10], consists of an installation of 15 black-and-white *Fig.* 10 *see pp.* 62 f.
photographs all of the same size and taken in Berlin, apart from two taken
in Dresden. Although some of them have been shown and published before,
the arrangement the artist has devised for *Time Travels* is new. These photographs are more than just an archeological inventory[40] or a social documentary,[41] accompanied by place and date rather than programmatic titles;
with these, as Döbert writes about Hauswald's exhibition in Jena in 2007,[42]
the seemingly long gone GDR lives on;[43] Rathenow and Hauswald represent
the past, make it alive again, disturbing those viewers for whom the past is
gone.[44] Critically seen, the photographer treats the past 'like a ventriloquist
manipulates its dummy', as Ines Weiman argues in a different context.[45]

Six of the 15 photographs depict the Brandenburg Gate (specifically the
Pariser Platz in front of the east side of the Brandenburg Gate), the symbol
and centre of Berlin and for many that of a new Germany. The view of the
gate is always from the east to the west, reflecting the photographer's East
German identity as living and working in the former GDR. The photograph
Brandenburg Gate, Berlin 22 December 1989 [*Fig.*11] in the centre is taken on *Fig.* 11 *see pp.* 62 f.
thc day of its official reopening after being shut and barricaded over almost
three decades. The reopening was watched by thousands of people, who
spilled on to the city's streets cheering in the pouring rain to watch the historic
ceremony in which Helmut Kohl, West German Chancellor at the time, walked
through the gate to be greeted by the East German Prime Minister Hans
Modrow. This event effectively ended the division of East and West Germany,
which was still in place in 1982, the year in which the photograph below
entitled *Brandenburg Gate, Berlin 1982* [*Fig.*12] was taken, depicting the long- *Fig.* 12 *see pp.* 62 f.
ing of those from the East for the West and reminding the viewer of a past
desire that has become reality. This photograph had been published in
1987[46] with the following text by Rathenow (cited in English after the 2005
edition), which captures the atmosphere of the Brandenburg Gate there and
then: 'The Brandenburg Gate is the only place where anyone may look at
and photograph the border without attracting attention. Rabbits hop over the
green areas in the prohibited zone.'[47]

The photograph at the top named after the square *Pariser Platz, Berlin
2005* [*Fig.*13], depicts the Brandenburg Gate in 2005, indicating that the story *Fig.* 13 *see pp.* 62 f.
does not end in 1989; the back of a living sculpture imitating the Statue of

Fig. 14 *see page* 63

Liberty is depicted in front of an open-air exhibition of the Brandenburg Gate, bringing to life its appearance just after the Second World War – the photographs mounted on large boards are visited by a number of summer-clothed tourists. Here photography is self-referential, but even more so in *Brandenburg Gate, Berlin 2005* [*Fig.* 14], which shows the mounted photographs solely in close-up. The living sculpture is not only an indexical sign for the temporaneity of the photographed scene, but also invites the viewer to draw parallels between the Statue of Liberty, the iconic celebratory American symbol for freedom, individuality and successful market economy, and the Brandenburg Gate, in front of which many speeches abouth achieving such values for the East were given. One of the most famous was by Ronald Reagan, who challenged the Soviet Union on 12 June 1987 with these words: 'Mr Gorbachev, tear down this wall!' Indeed, the wall came down, the gate still stands, in front of which the living Statue of Liberty in the photograph shows its bottom to those visitors approaching the gate from the east.

Fig. 16 *see pp.* 63
and 66 *f.*

Centre stage in *Brandenburg Gate, Berlin 2005* [*Fig.* 16] is a camera with delayed action shutter release pointed at a man posing in front of the Brandenburg Gate, which in this context has been commodified, becoming a tourist attraction, instead of symbolizing a higly politicized site. While the image discussed before [*Fig.* 14] represents the self-referentiality of the medium, this photograph is self-referential as regards the act of taking a photograph. It does not capture an object but rather the process of creating a self-portrait – again fixed into a medium, which seemingly takes time out of the equation, a topic to which I will return below.

Fig. 15 *see page* 63

The Brandenburg Gate forms the backdrop of a number of staged exhibitions, such as shown in *Brandenburg Gate, Berlin 2000* [*Fig.* 15]. The numerous white and black bears are arranged in strict order. The bears refer to the Berlin bear, depicted on the city crest of Berlin adopted for the whole of Berlin since 1990. Astrid Kuhlmey, who reviewed this photograph when it was published in *Gewendet*, has dismissed it as naïve, particularly when compared with those photographs referring to the time before 1989, such as

Fig. 12 *see pp.* 62 *f.*

Brandenburg Gate, Berlin 1982 [*Fig.* 12].[48] Such an interpretation overlooks the similarity between the lined-up bears on one side and the mass-produced

Fig. 17 *see page* 62

Trabis on the far right [*Fig.* 17] and the marching Soviets in the middle of the

Fig. 18 *see page* 62

next row [*Fig.* 18] in this installation [*see pp.* 64 *f.*]. What is critiqued (and equated) is the conformity propagated both in the GDR and in post-Communist Germany.

The pictures on the far right continue the Berlin stories into the postmodern: The Potsdamer Platz and the Alexanderplatz, two famous squares, are shown as places of temporaneity as in *Potsdamer Platz, Berlin 2005*

Fig. 19 *see page* 63

[*Fig.* 19], and individuality and free play as in both works entitled *Alexander-*

Figs. 20 *and* 21
see page 63

platz, Berlin 2006 [*Figs.* 20 and 21].[49] These photographs, as Hauswald's other pictures remind us, will also soon be stories of the past.

Fascinated by the Alexanderplatz, in 2007 Hauswald published a book dedicated to and entitled *Alexanderplatz, Berlin*, which includes photographs from before and after 1989 together with essays by 14 authors.[50] Both photographs entitled *Alexanderplatz, Berlin 2006* in the installation *Time Travels* feature the square as a loud and exhilarating place with dealers and street performers offering their goods. For Hauswald it is not a beautiful but a 'magic' place;[51] it has even been described as a place where many who know the literary importance of it (particularly through Döblin's novel *Berlin Alexanderplatz*) experience a culture shock when visiting.[52] Because of its large size – 80,000 square metres after its redesign in 1969, which included the erection of Walter Wornacka's so-called *Fountain of Friendship between Peoples*[53] as depicted on the bottom photograph [*Fig.*21] – the square was used to propagate the GDR's international credentials, although people experienced it as empty ('apart from wind, not much happened there', according to Hauswald).[54] In 1989, however, it became the meeting place for demonstrations against the forged local elections of 7 May of the same year.[55] For Markus Deggerich and Peter Wensierski, critics of Hauswald's book, it forms the most Eastern and honest face of the city in contrast to the Potsdamer Platz [*Fig.*19], which is a symbol of the collapse of the GDR in 1989, becoming the biggest construction site in any European city in the 1990s. Having vanished under massive skyscrapers (many built in a post-modern style), it probably represents the most Western face of Berlin, epitomizing the erasing of memory, which Ines Weizman names among the practices of German reunification.[56]

Fig. 21 *see page* 63

Fig. 19 *see page* 63

In stark contrast to these is the exact opposite side of the installation, which displays photographs taken before 1989. Cars and people in rank and file are ridiculed in *Berlin 1 May 1987* [*Fig.* 22] showing the ease with which such orderly behaviour is brought to an end, exposing it as 'unnatural.' *Berlin 1 May 1989* [*Fig.* 23][57] was taken only a few months before the collapse of the very state which was celebrated on that day, mocking the GDR state, its ideologies and cultural forms. It goes without saying that these photographs from the former GDR form a counterpart to the then official photojournalist press.

Fig. 22 *see page* 62

Fig. 23 *see page* 62

Underground Line A, Berlin 1986 [*Fig.* 24] is a photographic character study of individuals and as such anti-Communist, since it fashions the opposite of the communal, the collective, the public. In East German newspapers, reviewers of Hauswald's exhibitions usually comment on the unspectacular depicted by the photographer.[58] Barbara Glasser believes that this was a result of Hauswald's job as telegram boy in the GDR.[59] As such, he went to the courtyards, getting to know, in her words, the unspectacular life of simple citizens.[60] For this photograph, also entitled *Feierabend in der U-Bahn* (After Work in the Tube),[61] Hauswald took six shots. He reports that none of the three portrayed moved between taking each shot, reminding him of the three monkeys of which one does not see, the other does not hear and the third does not say anything.[62]

Fig. 24 *see pp.* 62 *f. and* 68 *f.*

Schlossplatz, Berlin 1982 [*Fig.* 17], showing a couple close to each other among numerous rows of East German Trabis, is probably the only one which depicts nostalgia for an era that is gone, often called *Ostalgie* (nostalgia for the East). It might represent one of those photographs which Döbert had in mind when writing about the exhibition in Jena in 2007: The photographs are

Fig. 17 *see page* 62

often rosy memories of a GDR which was probably not only black-and-white.[63]

Figs. 18 *and* 25 *see pp.* 62 *and* 64

The pair of photographs depicting the frieze of the Procession of the Dukes, which is at the back of the Royal Mews in Dresden, is taken from the same angle; the photograph at the bottom, *Procession of the Dukes, Dresden 1984* [*Fig.* 18], shows marching Soviet police in 1984, while the one at the top, *Procession of the Dukes, Dresden 2005* [*Fig.* 25], depicts a group of photographing tourists 21 years later. These two pictures encompass in some ways what Hauswald showed in the other photographs of Berlin, the before and after, but probably more pointedly, with little consideration of the processes in between.

Most of the photographs seem to be snapshots telling subjective stories. They evoke memory 'in its distance to the present' and thus create what Weizman considers as necessary for critique in general, 'an "outside" from where it is possible to sharply observe, reflect, destabilize and transgress the present.'[64] The 'outside' is the gap between each of these photographs, which can be interpreted as the Derridarian void, the unsayable; it represents the space full of tension, where the spectator experiences mourning, becomes disturbed, is reminded of old hopes and new illusions and thus begins processes of overcoming.

Fig. 26 *see page* 77

Sándor Pinczehelyi's contribution *Almost 30 Years* consists of two Pop Art inspired panels, of which one originates from 1973 and the other from 2002 [*Fig.* 26]. The first panel was produced during a time when the artist, influenced by the neo-geometry of the Pécs Workshop, to which Ferenc Ficzek, Károl Halász and Károly Kismányoki also belonged,[65] was particularly interested in symbols, such as the communist sickle and hammer as used here, but also five-pointed stars, as depicted in other works such as the *Star*

Fig. 27

(*Cobblestone*) of 1973 [*Fig.* 27].[66] In contrast to Zyśko, however, he represented them with an ironic undertone; the pose (crossed arms) in which he holds the hammer and sickle may be read as a reference to Egyptian representations,[67] but it also means in Hungarian 'sh.'.[68] For the artist, the gesture constituted an attempt to remove all the unnecessary political overtones that these symbols had acquired. He felt that he had to offload the ideological burden that they had collected and then reinstate them in their fundamental role,[69] arranging them in a way that they are almost organic parts of the body. As Hegyi Lóránd has argued, the work becomes then an allegory for the way in which political reality was inseparably united with the individual fates.[70]

Fig. 1

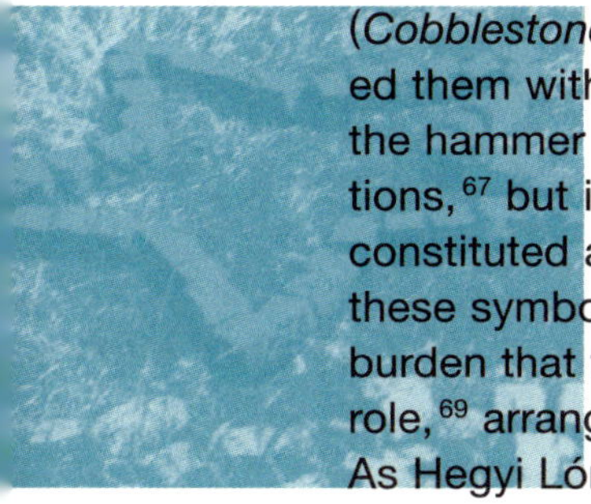

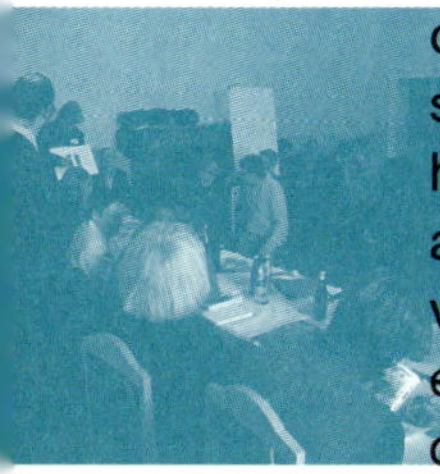

The silkscreen's counterpart of 2002 depicts the artist in black-and-white and without the communist symbols (and this absence is very much felt), but still holding his hands in the same position as in 1973, indicating his equal disinterest in or even aversion to the present. As Pinczehelyi said at the workshop in Poland in March 2007 [*Fig.* 1], he not only dislikes the past, but also his own works, and would like to experience new situations and find new answers.[71] Against this longing for the new, the paired self-portraits draw the viewer back, indexing continuity at the same time: The same person depicted on the portraits bridges not only the body's natural changes as a result of getting older, but also the Communist red-coloured lived ideology with the post-Communist black-and-white society. The private and the public may change, but it is the individual, the person, who takes centre-stage. Similar to Hauswald, Pinczehelyi uses the technique of contrast of before and after paradoxically, however, to counter-argue the concept of contrast.

For Ulf Göpfert, the purpose of remembering is to learn from it in order to avoid other dictatorships.[72] His contribution, entitled *Individuality Versus Dictatorship* of 2008 [*Fig. 28*], consists of a tank which functions as an icon *Fig. 28 see pp. 58 f.* for those historical events in which tanks have been used, such as the 1953 unarmed workers' demonstration in East Berlin, the 1956 Hungarian revolution against the Communist government and the 1968 Prague Spring liberaliza-tion reform attempts. The tank also stands for those powers in dictatorships which are veiled, hitting unexpectedly – like a tank, camouflaged to create disaster in a moment of surprise. Painted vibrantly in acrylic colours, the work is rather playful, which suggests an influence of Western Postmodern-ism. Indeed, Göpfert claims to have started to paint again after seeing a Pop Art show in Leipzig in 1983 (he had given up painting to work as a furniture restorer).[73] In his introduction to the catalogue published on the occasion of Göpfert's exhibition at the Stadtarchiv in Dresden in 2008, Jördis Lademann cites Willy Wolff, the *homo ludens* among artists in Dresden whose work has responded to American Abstract Colour Field Painting and Pop Art col-lages, as one of Göpfert's influences.[74] Moreover, acrylic colours as such can *Fig. 29* also be seen in contrast to grey, said to be the dominant colour of the GDR, the proletarian GDR,[75] and as an influence from the West since the 1980s, when such synthetic colours started to be available in tubes in the GDR.[76] For the artist, the colours and designs are an expression of individuality, coun-teracting uniformity and thus dictatorship, because to him dictatorship is the oppression of many individuals in favour of few.[77] Seen from within a post-modern perspective, the colourful multi-patterned design attempting to hide the object's violent powers is only invisible in a 'multi-coloured', non-deter-mined environment. Does not this context put the emphasis on the form, the armoured tank? Even if it looks like a toy rather than a Soviet, U.S. or UN tank prepared to go into action and battle, the tension – if not paradox – between play and brutality, joy and violence is obvious. The use of an object of military power also strongly voices the monstrosity of the indistinguishable in a postmodern world, in which the individual can only survive with a raised canon [*Fig. 29*]. For the artist, the answer lies in art, which also explains his involvement in cultural politics after the fall of the wall:[78] 'Art is the tension between individuality and submission, singularity and domination of the means.'[79]

Zbyněk Benýšek contributed a panel in which he depicts the dis-interest in the past in the Czech Republic in the mid-1990s. In *Prague Buffet* of 1995 [*Fig. 30*], people in a small restaurant do not seem to watch Pier *Fig. 30 see pp. 50 f.* Paolo Pasolini's cinematic adaptation of the life of Jesus in *The Gospel Ac-cording to St. Matthew*, running on a TV screen placed among them. Likewise they seem oblivious to the surreal but realistically painted hunt of a large vulture-like bird. Indifferent to surreal and mediated cruelty, people are only concerned about their daily worries and the banality of life.

Fig. 31 *see page* 80

Fig. 32

Zyśko's installation *Obelisk* of 2007 [*Fig.* 31] alludes to the Roman invasions resulting in a vast empire. According to Plutarch (Cicero 22.2), *Vixerunt*, the text on the obelisk [*Fig.* 32], is an expression used by Cicero to summarize his report of the execution of several of Cataline's followers to the Senate. It means that they have lived and was supposed to guard against ill fortune by avoiding the direct mention of death. The language supports the pointer to the Roman Empire, but also hints at the artist's home country, Poland, in which the Catholic Church played an important role in the Communist era and is still one of the dominating forces, as outlined above. The paradoxical phrase is also highlighted by the material. The obelisk, made of an iron frame covered by a canvas sleeve and surrounded by sawdust, shows the fragility of monumentality but also the fragility of overcoming dictatorial hegemonies. *Vixerunt* – these found an end, but their ideologies may still be alive.

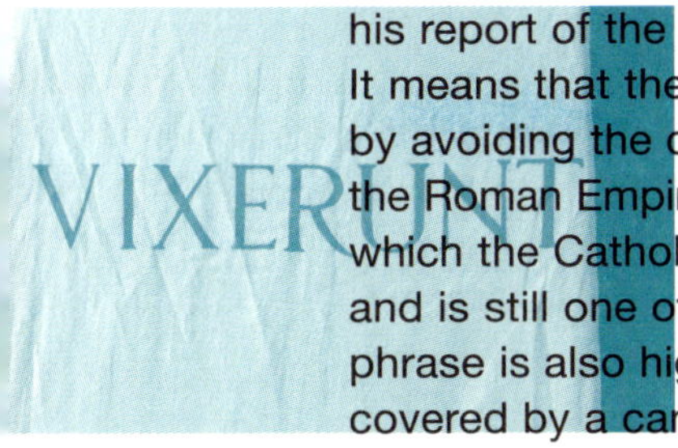

Fig. 33 *see page* 70

Seemingly more stable, although tantalizing in other ways, is Silvestro Lodi's installation *Hanging History – Stock of History* of 2007-2008 [*Fig.* 33]. The work addresses the various ways in which history can be dealt with, playing with the word 'hanging': the past can be hanged, explained dead, or it can be hung to be stored – forgotten or remembered.[80] The artist uses a clothes hanger similar to those in domestic households from which nine cardboard designs resembling ties, male symbols of etiquette and power, fashion and expression, dangle. Although displayed in order, these can get mixed up with little outside force, just as events can change the history of a country. Which of the templates will prevail and come top of the others? Which of the 'Stock of History' will remain on the shelves, which will be sold and which will be worn? As Massimo Donà comments on other hangers produced by Lodi: 'His works are like clothes hanging and waiting to be worn; like clothes caught in the second before they are used.'[81] As an artwork, the ties of *Hanging History* remain in this waiting position; furthermore, they remind the viewer of mass production and relate to commerce, since the objects are referred to in the title as 'stock'. The history with which the artist is concerned is the male-dominated, economico-national dictatorical past of the countries involved in the project 'Overcoming Dictatorships.' Each of the ties represents one of these countries, and one is dedicated to the EU.

The tie on the outside stands for the Czech Republic. Lodi refers to its present (the blue, white and red of the national flag) and its past under the influence of National Socialism [*Fig.* 33].[82] It bears a portrait of Reinhard Heydrich, the so-called 'protector' of Bohemia and Moravia from 1941 until his assassination in 1942. Appointed to chair the Wannsee conference of 1942 and considered as a possible successor by Hitler, he is for the artist the paradigm of the criminality of a dictatorship.[83] The tie next to this one is dedicated to Romania, represented by the colour of its flag and a head with 'vin in 5 minutes' on the upper half and Romanian writing at the bottom; the back features the hand of Ceauşescu. It is followed by Germany, with the former GDR flag on one side and that of the FRG on the reverse; for the artist, the country is still divided.[84] Since the work is about representing dictatorships, the artist also depicts the other half of former ČSSR, Slovakia, with its national flag and a full-length portrait of Karl Rahm, commandant of the Theresienstadt concentration camp. In the central position is the tie dedicated to the EU, with the golden stars on a blue background and, in reference to communism, with blue stars on a red background. The EU is depicted as central, but not as dominating the other countries, since the size of the tie is the same.[85] It is followed by the flag for the UK: one side bears the Union flag representing the United Kingdom and Northern Ireland, the other shows a detail of the flag in black-and-white with a woman's eyes. The next is dedicated to Fascist Italy, showing a waving Mussolini above the colours of the Italian flag. The other side represents a three-quarter-length portrait of the waving Mussolini in black-and-white. The last but one tie is occupied by the tricolour of red, white and green of the Hungarian flag on both sides of the tie and again a waving hand on the front. The last one (or first, depending on the perspective) represents Poland, with the colours of the flag and 'Polo' on one side and a full-length portrait of Rudolf Höss, commandant of Auschwitz concentration camp from 1940 to 1942, on the other, reminding of the Nazi period.[86] With a mixture of colours and symbols of flags as well as portraits of people who the artist considers as contributors to the Holocaust, dictators or representatives of a dictatorial system, the work offers possibilities as to how to deal with history. For the artist, it is down to the individual to remember or forget, to mix up the stories of each country and to compare them or treat each one separately.[87] Consequently, he contributes a similar hanger entitled *My Own Hanging History – My Stock of History*, 2008 [*Fig.* 35][88], which refers to the other hanger not only in title but also in style, technique and use of some of the pictures, such as that of Reinhard Heydrich (here, however, portrayed with a long nose ridiculing the person in uniform), and symbols, such as the hand. The artist used to say that an artist's hand thinks.[89] Here, however, it has become a metaphor of the dictator's ideology. The hanger also bears references to the artist's personal and subjective experiences, such as his walk through Berlin (no. 6 from right) and his memories of his grandfather, Giovanni, a tailor, in whose shop the artist learned to draw as a child (no. 1 from right) and whose influence can be seen in Lodi's use of dashes on the ties which look like cut-out lines of dressmaker paper charts.

Fig. 35 *see page* 71

Apart from Benýšek in *Saint Sebastian* of 1997 [*Fig.* 7], none of the artists has referred explicitly to the physical danger, mistreatment and cruelty experienced under dictatorships, focusing rather on social and economic pressures. This is surprising, since Benýšek was not the only one to suffer under Communism. Born in Prostějov (Moravia) in 1949 and moving to Prague after his training as an artist at the Brno School of Applied Arts, Benýšek was persecuted because in January 1977 he signed Charter 77, a document which gave its name to the most prominent dissident group of the Czechoslovak Communist government, with Václav Havel as one of the founding members. As a result, Benýšek emigrated to Vienna in 1982, from where he returned to Prague in 1992.

Fig. 7 *see page* 49

Hauswald, born in Radebeul, near Dresden, in 1954, had to be very careful when taking photographs in Berlin, to which he had moved in 1977. These were not published in the GDR, but appeared in West Germany in journals such as *GEO, Stern* and *ZEIT Magazin* [90] and in book format published by Piper in Munich in 1987 (at the time of Berlin's 750th anniversary).[91] The book, with text by Lutz Rathenow, at the time a GDR dissident, and photographs of everyday life in East Berlin, was reissued in 2005 with a different selection of photographs both on the cover and in the book. In the preface, Rathenow mentions that he and Hauswald emptied an apartment in a rundown part of a residential building and plastered it with Hauwald's photos so they could discuss the selection for the book.[92] He reports that the photographs of this mini-exhibition 'mysteriously vanished without a trace from Hauswald's archive and have never resurfaced.'[93] An answer to the mystery may be found in the reception of the book by the GDR government. The book was not openly defamatory; the photographs *Brandenburg Gate, Berlin 1982* [*Fig.* 12] and *Underground Line A, Berlin 1986* [*Fig.* 24] included in *Time Travels* of 2008, also appeared in the book. However, the German title *Ost-Berlin* (East Berlin), which was used officially in West Germany and unofficially in the GDR for the Eastern part of Berlin until reunification (officially East Berlin was 'Berlin' – the capital of the GDR), attracted attention presumably because of its non-heroic approach, in contrast to those official GDR photographs, which rather cultivated the myth of the socialist proletarian state.[94] Rathenow, having been able to scrutinize secret Stasi files in the meantime, cites a letter from Kurt Hager, the leading GDR politician for cultural issues, to Erich Mielke, GDR Minister of State Security at the time the book appeared in 1987: 'The suitability of instigating proceedings through the director of GDR copyright law, as proposed by you, must be thoroughly reconsidered. It would be better, if, after the book's publication, the customs authorities were to instigate a criminal investigation due to customs and currency offences.'[95]

Figs. 12 *and* 24
see pp. 62 *f.*

Although the authors' description of the Berlin book as part of the Cold War may have been a little too pretentious, it nevertheless instigated 'an expert group [which] compiled a report of many pages' and the concluding verdict by Mielke: 'The proposal that the Ministry of Foreign Affairs employ suitable means to point out to agencies in Bonn that the publication of the book by Rathenow and Hauswald in Piper Verlag is an unfriendly act contravening the cultural exchange between the GDR and the FRG as laid out in the culture convention, meets with my approval. I will arrange for the Ministry of Foreign Affairs to instruct comrade Moldt accordingly.'[96]

According to the authors, the book was sold out within a year, but – and this may demonstrate Piper's loyalty to the FRG government – not reissued despite its success in terms of sales. It was Harenberg in Dortmund which produced a bibliophile edition in 1989, which again sold out in a year.[97]

Because of his unheroic photographs of life in East Berlin, Hauswald experienced surveillance, house searches and interrogations.[98] Altogether, his Stasi file weighed seven kilos.[99] He earned his living by being a telegram messenger, restorer and photo-lab assistant and exhibited in youth clubs, rooms in churches and private flats. Although without doubt, the major reason for this was political, Hauswald's photographs were aesthetically untimely in the 1980s, a period in which GDR photography ignored social reality and concentrated on art photography, paying no attention to social documentary photography.[100] In the new Germany, however, Hauswald became officially recognized receiving the *Bundesverdienstkreuz* in 1997 (Order of Merit of the Federal Republic of Germany).

In contrast to Hauswald, Sándor Pinczehelyi, born in 1946 in Szigetvár (Hungary), was already established as an artist in Hungary, particularly since the 1970s, a time when the first reforms took place which eventually led to the opening of the borders to Austria in 1989. He was not only director of the Pécs Art City Gallery from 1977 to 1999, but was also commissioned to represent Hungary at the Venice Biennale in 1988. However, even he suffered repressive measures, his art being critical of the government. He participated in an exhibition which had been forbidden because of allegedly being too much influenced by the West with a surrealist montage of a photographic self-portrait entitled *XYZ* of 1973 [*Fig.* 37], in which his hand goes in and out of his chest, referencing to the moment when Christ showed his crucifixion wounds to the apostles in order to make them believe that he had survived. Although in 1973, Pinczehelyi referred openly to suffering, being torn apart but with a strong self-belief, he has chosen not to contribute this or a similar works to the project 'Overcoming Dictatorships.' The underlying reason for not referring to the suffering under Communism in works produced or discussed in the project may well be because his experience is considered rather personal and sensitive. In addition, reflections of the past may also not always be as clear-cut as one would like them to be. This may also explain why questions of how to treat members of the former governments – as, for example, in Jens Rudolph's film *Staats_Sicherheit* of 2004 [*Fig.* 38], shot in the Stasi-Unterlagen-Behörde in Berlin and problematizing the treatment of members of the East German secret service after German reunification – have also not been an issue in discussions.

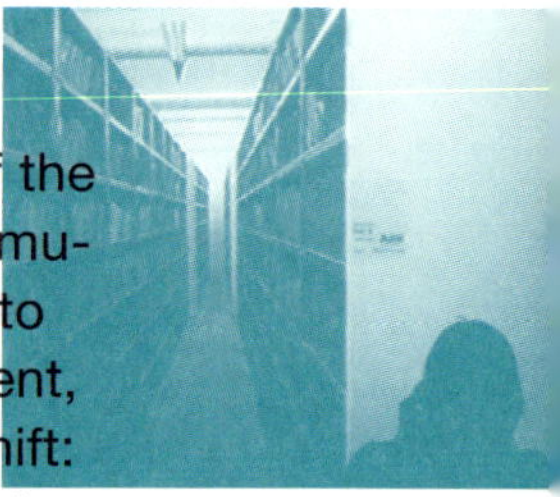

In 1999, David Elliott observed that 'in the majority (but not all) of the twenty two countries [participating in the exhibition *After the Wall*] Communism (Marxist-Leninism) is an ideology which has been firmly consigned to the past and was then regarded as an irrelevance, if not an embarrassment, to the present and future.'[101] Now, nearly a decade later, we can see a shift: processes such as mourning, remembering, critical reading of the present in the light of the past imply that the past – including its ideology – is far from being gone. On the contrary, as, for example, the success of Hauswald and Rathenow's 2005 book (published now in its third edition) proves, perspectives have changed. These subjective searches for the past may also be read as a counter-process to the treatment of history in the former Communist countries; according to Marina Gržinić, the 'whole socialist machine was aimed at neutralizing the side effects of a relevant interpretation of its reality and of art production, at covering up history, effacing and renaming it.'[102] Overcoming is in the process of being turned over: reflective not-yet-belonging is becoming an appropriation of the 'now.' This may arguably also

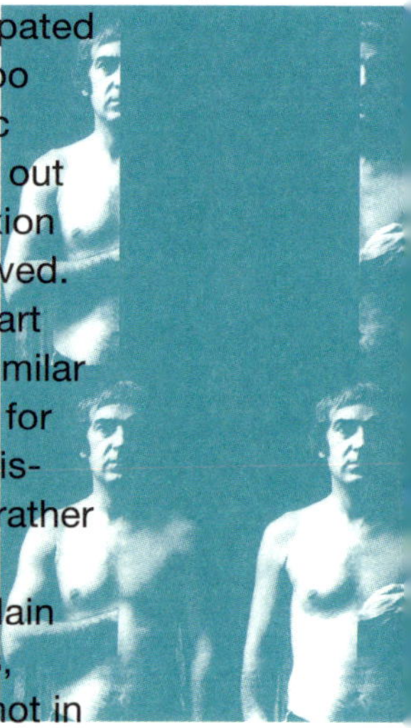

Fig. 37

Fig. 38

be seen as a logical step for some after a state of 'normality', mainly understood in economic terms, to which the Soviet bloc states returned after 1989, as proposed by Bojana Pejić for the period until the end of the 1990s.[103] While the 1990s were probably more concerned with forgetting the past and the sheer enthusiasm, dreams and hopes for the new,[104] the 'Overcoming Dictatorships' project and its outcome may be taken as emblematic for a slightly different approach in the middle of the first decade of the new millennium characterized by an imperative re-reading of the past. In reference to Martin Walser one may, however, critically ask to what extent the works discussed above – and probably the project as such – ritualize and instrumentalize the memory of Communism,[105] instead of using iconoclasm or letting slip the past, hiding (as with all of the Nazi and most of the Communist memorials)[106] or erasing it (as in the 1990s), as a way of dealing with dictatorial periods.

[24] See, for example, Cristina Palamares, *The Quest For Survival After Franco,* Brighton, 2004; Merry M. Pawlowski (ed.), *Virginia Woolf and Fascism. Resisting the Dictators' Seduction,* Houndsmills, 2001; Boris Groys, *The Total Art of Stalinism. Avant-Garde, Aesthetic Dictatorship, and Beyond,* Princeton, 1992; José Antonio Maravall, *Dictatorship and Political Dissent: Workers and Students in Franco's Spain,* London, 1978; Ian Kershaw (ed.), *Stalinism and Nazism. Dictatorship in Comparison,* Cambridge, 1997; Emily Braun, *Mario Sironi and Italian Modernism. Art and Politics Under Fascism,* Cambridge, 2000; *Art and Propaganda in the Twentieth Century. The Political Image in the Age of Mass Culture,* London, 1997; Dawn Ades (ed.), *Art and Power. Europe Under the Dictators 1930-45,* exh. cat., London, Hayward Gallery, 1995; Andrew Hewitt, *Fascist Modernism. Aesthetics, Politics, and the Avant-garde,* Stanford, 1993; Igor Golomstock, *Totalitarian Art in the Soviet Union, the Third Reich, Fascist Italy and People's Republic of China,* London, 1990.

[25] See, for example, Peter Baehr *et al.* (eds.), *Dictatorship in History and Theory. Bonapartism, Caesarism, and Totalitarianism,* Cambridge, 2004; Todd Porterfield and Susan L. Siegfried, *Staging Empire. Napoleon, Ingres, and David,* Pennsylvania, 2006. The term has also entered social areas: George J. Barnsby, *Dictatorship of the Bourgeoisie. Social Control in the Nineteenth Century Black Country,* London, 1972; Siegfried, Susan, *The Art of Louis-Leopold Boilly. Modern Life in Napoleonic France,* New Haven, 1995; Edgar Munhall, 'Portraits of Napoleon', *Yale French Studies,* no. 26, 1960, 3-20; Timothy Wilson-Smith, *Napoleon and His Artists,* London, 1996; Malcolm Croke, *Napoleon Comes to Power. Democracy and Dictatorship in Revolutionary France,* Cardiff, 1998.

[26] See, for example, Michael McFaul, *Between Dictatorship and Democracy. Russian Post-Communist Political Reform,* Washington, 2004. For those countries involved in the project, see the titles in the bibliography.

[27] The 50th Venice Biennial was dedicated to 'Dreams and Conflicts: The Dictatorship of the Viewer' (14 June to 2 Nov. 2003) which received much criticism. For curatorship, see, for example, Sabine B. Vogel, 'Biennalen – kittet mellan demokrati och diktatur', *Paletten,* vol. 270-271, 2008, 6-11. Furthermore, titles such as Patrick Higgins, *Heterosexual Dictatorship,* London, 1996 use the term in entirely different contexts.

[28] See Norberto Bobbio, *Democracy and Dictatorship. The Nature and Limits of State Power,* Oxford, 1989 (first published in Italian in 1980), 159. See also Daniel N. Nelson (ed.), *After Authoritarianism. Democracy or Disorder?,* London, 1995 and Hellmut Lehmann-Haupt, *Art Under a Dictatorship,* New York et al., 1954.

[29] See Norberto Bobbio, *ibid.,* 159 and 166. See also Gerhard Besier, *Das Europa der Diktaturen. Eine neue Geschichte des 20. Jahrhunderts,* Munich, 2006, particularly the last chapter, where he discusses both Communist and Fascist regimes under authoritarian systems with reference to Max Weber and Wolfgang Merkel (see 698f.). He argues that the difference between autocracy and democracy is clearer than that between its subtypes. Within the Marxist framework, it also served as a positive hallmark: the 'dictatorship of the proletariat' (see, for example, John Ehrenberg, *The Dictatorship of the Proletariat,* New York et al., 1992). For contemporary sources, see also Karl Kautsky, *Demokratie oder Diktatur,* Berlin, 1918 and Carl Schmitt, *Die Diktatur. Von den Anfängen des modernen Souveränitätsgedankens bis zum proletarischen Klassenkampf,* Berlin, 2006 (first edition in 1921).

[30] Marius Oprea in March 2006, cited in *The Institute,* pamphlet of the Institute for the Investigation of Communist Crimes in Romania, n.d. (published by the Institute).

[31] See Vlad Nancă in Barbara Lubich, Workshop 2 in Wałbrzych (Poland), 30 March to 1 April 2007, DVD, unpublished (archive material of the project, TU Dresden).

[32] See, for example, Naomi Klein, *No-Logo: No Space, No Choice, No Jobs,* London, 2001.

[33] See Zbyněk Benýšek below under 'In the Artists' Voices'.

[34] See Tomás Pospiszyl, 'Jakub Hošek', Suzanne Cotter, Andrew Nairne and Victoria Pomery (eds.), *Arrivals,* 96.

[35] See Zbigniew Czop in Barbara Lubich, Workshop 2 in Wałbrzych (Poland).

36   See, for example, Karol Sauerland, 'Die Rolle der katholischen Kirche Polens', *Kirchliche Zeitgeschichte/ Contemporary Church History*, vol. 2, 2007, 288-297, 295. He also refers to the seminal work published in underground by Adam Michnik, *Die Kirche und die polnische Linke. Von der Konfrontation zum Dialog*, Munich, 1980.

37   Gerhard Besier, 'Einleitung', *Kirchliche Zeitgeschichte/Contemporary Church History*, vol. 20, 2007, 288-297 and 217-223, 219.

38   See Harald Hauswald and Lutz Rathenow, *Gewendet. Vor und nach dem Mauerfall. Fotos und Texte aus dem Osten*, Berlin, 2006, and *Ost-Berlin. Leben for dem Mauerfall. Life Before the Wall Fell*, Berlin, 2005.

39   See below ('Biographies of the Artists').

40   See Giovanni di Lorenzo, 'Bevor alles gleich war', *Zeitmagazin*, no. 46, 8 Nov. 2007, 42-51, 43.

41   See Katharina Lenski, 'Ewige DDR', *Deutschland Archiv*, no. 3, 2007, 401-403, 401 and Bernd Lindner, 'Ein Land – zwei Bilderwelten. Fotografie und Öffentlichkeit in der DDR', Karin Hartewig and Alf Lüdtke (eds.), *Die DDR im Bild*, 189-206.

42   Hauswald's exhibition in Jena in 2007 entitled *Die ewige DDR* (the Eternal GDR) received much criticism. The *Ostthüringer Zeitung* (20 Feb. 2007) reports under the heading 'Von "großartig" bis "mies"' that two-third of the entries in the guest book of the exhibition were negative. The comments suggest that the reason for criticizing the images was because they were shown under that particular title. The exhibition also included Hauswald's *Underground Line A, Berlin* of 1986 (see Fig. 24).

43   Frank Döbert, 'Glänzende Fotos, spitze Feder', *Ostthüringer Zeitung*, 31 Jan. 2007, no page ('Lokales').

44   Stefanie Grießbach, 'Lebensbilder', *Ostthüringische Zeitung*, 12 Feb. 2007, no page ('Kultur').

45   Ines Weizman, 'Critique Without Memory, or Memory Without Critique', Ilina Koralova (ed.), *Against. Within*, 21-35, 30.

46   See Harald Hauswald and Lutz Rathenow, *Ostberlin. Die andere Seite einer Stadt in Texten und Bildern*, Munich, 1987, 69. Here it appeared next to three others depicting East Berlin places: the Prussian eagle, a scene from the Družba feast (friendship feast) and a skyscraper façade decorated with a pigeon and the words in German 'Berlin. City of Peace.' In this context, the barricaded Brandenburg Gate forms a direct contrast to peace and friendship.

47   Lutz Rathenow in Harald Hauswald and Lutz Rathenow, *Ost-Berlin*, 54.

48   Astrid Kuhlmey, '*Gewendet* [review of the book by Hauswald and Rathenow]', *Brennpunkt*, no. 1, 2007, 25f, 26.

49   Gisa Weszkalnys, 'The Disintegration of a Socialist Exemplar: Discourses on Urban Disorder in Alexanderplatz, Berlin', *Space & Culture*, no. 10, 2007, 207-230.

50   See Harald Hauswald, *Alexanderplatz. Fotografische und literarische Erinnerungen*, Berlin, 2007.

51   See Harald Hauswald, cited by Ingeborg Ruthe, 'Ein Narbengesicht, das östlichste, ehrlichste der Stadt', *Berliner Zeitung*, 16 Oct. 2007, no page and Harald Hauswald, 'Ein magischer Ort', Harald Hauswald, *Alexanderplatz*, 7.

52   See Markus Deggerich and Peter Wensierski, 'Das Narbengesicht', Harald Hauswald, *Alexanderplatz*, 39-42, 39.

53   In the 1970s, the fountain was also known as *Nuttenbrosche*, referring to the prostitutes who could be picked up there (see Uwe Kolbe, 'Halbsätze, dem Alexanderplatz hingeworfen', Harald Hauswald, *Alexanderplatz*, 101-102, 101).

54   See Harald Hauswald, 'Ein magischer Ort', Harald Hauswald, *Alexanderplatz*, 7.

55   See Thomas Brussig, 'Die Wahrheit der Bauchbinde', Harald Hauswald, Alexanderplatz, 15-18, 17.

56   See Ines Weizman, 'Critique Without Memory, or Memory Without Critique', 34.

57   For the preparation and celebration of 1 May in the GDR, see Hans-Hermann Hertle and Stefan Wolle, *Damals in der DDR. Der Alltag im Arbeiter- und Bauernstaat*, Munich, 2006, 312ff.

58   See, for example, Ulrike Merkel, 'Ewige DDR', *Ostthüringer Zeitung*, 23 Feb. 2007, no page ('Kultur').

59   For here and the following, see Barbara Glasser, 'Bilder erzählen kleine Geschichten', *Thüringische Landeszeitung*, 8 Feb. 2007, no page.

60   See *ibid*.

61   See Stefanie Grießbach, 'Lebensbilder', no page.

62   See Harald Hauswald, cited by Stefanie Grießbach, 'Lebensbilder', no page.

63   Frank Döbert, 'Glänzende Fotos, spitze Feder', no page.

64   See Ines Weizman, 'Critique Without Memory, or Memory Without Critique', 35.

65   See Gábor Andrási, 'The Seventies', Gábor Andrási, Gábor Pataki, György Szücs and András Zwickl (eds.) 33, see p. 70 *The History of Hungarian Art in the Twentieth Century*, 181-209, 204.

66   See Hegyi Lóránd, *Pinczehelyi*, Pécs, 1995, 4 and also Magdalena Radomska, 'Semantyczne pole minowe', *Art. Magazyn o sztuce*, no. 4, 2007, 22-25.

67   See Hegyi Lóránd, *Pinczehelyi*, 12.

68   See Email from Katalin Gádoros, 10 June 2007 to the author.

69   See Sándor Pinczehelyi below under 'In the Artists' Voices'.

70   See Hegyi Lóránd, *Pinczehelyi*, 12.

71   See Sándor Pinczehelyi in Barbara Lubich, Workshop 2 in Wałbrzych (Poland).

72   Ulf Göpfert in Barbara Lubich, Workshop 2 in Wałbrzych (Poland).

73   See below ('Biographies of the Artists'). Jördis Lademann, *Ulf Göpfert. Metamorphosen,* with an introduction by Jördis Lademann, exh. cat., Dresden, Stadtarchiv Dresden, 2007.

74   See *ibid.,* 7 (citing Armin Hauer, *Kunst in der DDR,* exh. cat., Berlin, Nationalgalerie, 2003, 172). Lademann refers to Wolff as someone who spent his life on the margins of the official Socialist Realist art market (see *ibid.*).

75   See Astrid Kuhlmey, '*Gewendet* [review of the book by Hauswald and Rathenow]', 25.

76   See Jördis Lademann, *Ulf Göpfert,* 7. In an interview with Lars von Töne ('Der erste Platz im Staate', Harald Hauswald, *Alexanderplatz,* 59-62, 60), the architect Roland Korn, instrumental in rebuilding the Alexanderplatz in 1966, also reports that pigments used for the window panes of a hotel built on the square had to be imported from the West, since the GDR industry was unable to produce them.

77   See Ulf Göpfert in Barbara Lubich, Workshop 3 in Ústí nad Labem (Czech Republic), 17 to 19 May 2007, DVD, unpublished (archive material of the project, TU Dresden) and Ulf Göpfert, Questionnaire (Answer to the question: What does 'overcoming dictatorships' mean to you?), April 2007, unpublished (archive material of the project, TU Dresden).

78   Lutz Vogel, First Mayor of Dresden in 2008, mentions Göpfert's achievements in his foreword to Jördis Lademann, *Ulf Göpfert,* no page; as head commissioner of culture and tourism he has been instrumental in restoring the Kulturrathaus in the Neustadt quarter in Dresden, an eighteenth-century building which has been used for cultural events since.

79   Göpfert in Wolfgang Boesner and Yvonne Schwarzer (eds.), *Künstler. Werk. Material. 77 Künstlerwege,* Witten, 2004, 146.

80   See Silvestro Lodi in Barbara Lubich, Workshop 3 in Ústí nad Labem (Czech Republic).

81   See Massimo Donà, 'Remembrance of Forgotten Music. The Impersonality of "Truth" in the Paintings of Silvestro Lodi', Silvestro Lodi, *Vibrazoni,* exh. cat., Vanezia, Galleria d'Arte l'Occhio, 2006, no page.

82   Notice the different order of the ties in the work (Fig. 33, see p. 70) and the schematic view of the ties (Fig. 34, see the following page). The following analysis refers to the art work.

83   See *ibid.*

84   See Silvestro Lodi in Barbara Lubich, Workshop 3 in Ústí nad Labem (Czech Republic).

85   Lodi's schematic view of the work (Fig. 34, see the following page) depicts the EU even not in such a central position.

86   See *ibid.*

87   See Silvestro Lodi in Barbara Lubich, Workshop 3 in Ústí nad Labem (Czech Republic).

88   Again notice the different order of the ties in the work (Fig. 35, see p. 71) and the schematic view (Fig. 36). And again, the analysis follows the illustration of the art work, not the scheme.

89   See for here and the following Silvestro Lodi, Email to the author, 30 March 2008.

90   See Giovanni di Lorenzo, 'Bevor alles gleich war', 43.

91   See Harald Hauswald and Lutz Rathenow, *Ost-Berlin. Die andere Seite einer Stadt in Texten und Bildern,* Munich, 1987. The book was reissued after the fall of the wall with different photographs on the cover and in the book as Harald Hauswald and Lutz Rathenow, *Ost-Berlin.* Most importantly, in terms of the photographs, the places were no longer explained, assuming a readership which would know East Berlin (although the text is now in English and German).

92   *Ibid.,* 8.

93   *Ibid.*

94   See Katharina Klotz, 'Foto – Montage – Plakat. Zur politischen Ikonographie der "sozialistischen Sichtagitation" in der frühen DDR', Karin Hartewig and Alf Lüdtke (eds.), *Die DDR im Bild,* 29-49.

95   Harald Hauswald and Lutz Rathenow, *Ost-Berlin,* 6.

96   Mielke, cited in Harald Hauswald and Lutz Rathenow, *Ost-Berlin,* Berlin, 2005, 6f. Rathenow reports that the book was 'understood as an expression of a new scene in Prenzlauer Berg and interpreted as a document of the increasing oppositional self-confidence in the GDR in general. Although deprived of the chance of placing announcements in the general press, over 700 persons came to the opening of a photo presentation with accompanying reading during the Protestant Church Congress in Berlin in 1988. I had my book fee – except for a small advance – paid into paperback editions of a few of my other books, which were smuggled over the border in several thousand copies. They were then sold or given away at readings, so that the existence of this Berlin book multiplied my West presence in the East in several ways.' (*ibid.,* 8).

97   See Harald Hauswald and Lutz Rathenow, *Ost-Berlin,* 7.

98   See Harald Hauswald in Stefanie Grießbach, 'Lebensbilder', no page and Christian Dorn, 'Leben vor dem Mauerfall', 84.

99   See Ulrike Merkel, 'Ewige DDR', no page.

100   See Karim Saab, 'Mit beseeltem Blick', *Die Märkische,* 4/5 Feb. 2006, no page.

101   David Elliott, 'Introduction', 011.

102   See Marina Gržinić, 'On the Re-Politicisation of Art Through Contamination', Irwin (ed.), *East Art Map,* 477-486, 484.

103   See Bojana Pejić, 'The dialectics of normality', 016-028. Zbigniew Czop also refers to building a society based on 'normality' (see Zbigniew Czop below under 'In the Artists' Voices'), so does Carl Tighe, *The Politics of Literature. Poland 1945-1989,* Cardiff, 1999, 338.

104   See, for example, Pavla Pecinkova, *Contemporary Czech Painting,* East Roseville, 1993, 17, who speaks of 'new possibilities and great dreams.'

105   Martin Walser, *Deutsche Sorgen,* Frankfurt, 1997. The same could be said of the so called Statue Park outside Budapest, which is an open space exhibition of Communist memorials removed from their pre-1989 location (see also its publication which is entitled Ákos Rétlhy (ed.), *Statue Park. Gigantic Monuments from the Age of Communist Dictatorship,* Budapest, no date and its website szoborpark.hu).

106   This approach was suggested for Heinrich Tüpke's mural painting at the Dresden University. See Karl-Siegbert Rehberg, Ideenkunst als Schlüssel der Gesellschaftsanalyse. Der Fall der DDR, conference paper, Overcoming Dictatorships. Intellettuali e Regimi, as part of the Workshop 6 in Trent (Italy), 9 to 10 May 2008.

Fig. 34

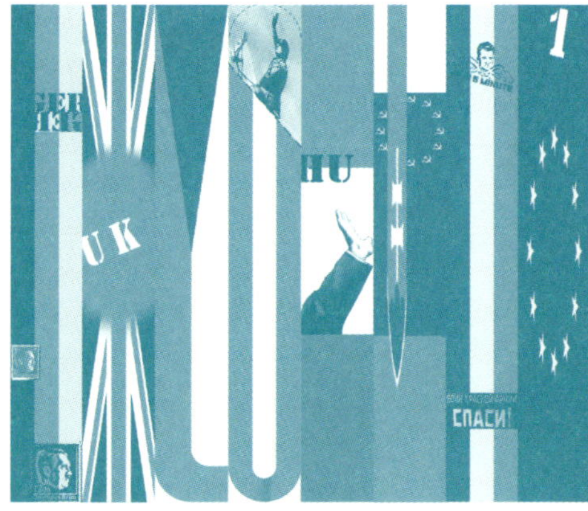

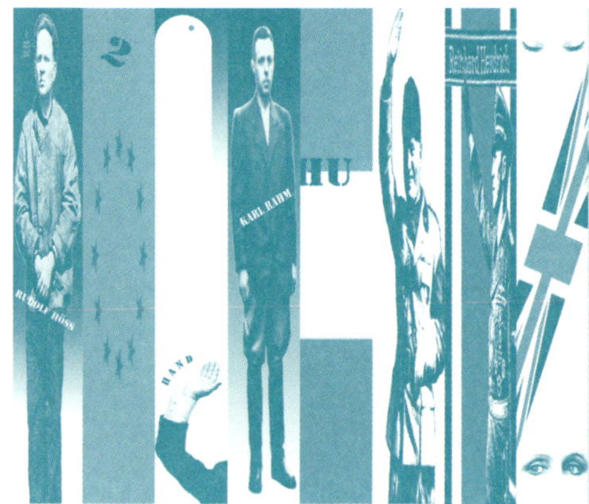

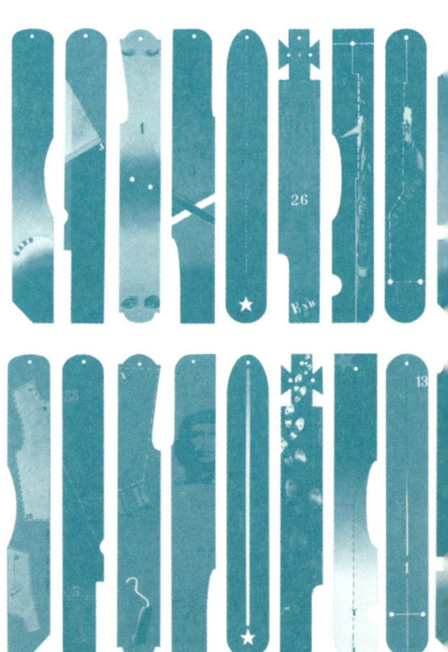

Fig. 36

2 New Dictatorships

In addition to the question of how to overcome dictatorships, the artists have been concerned about the forming of new ones in terms of economy, society and technology. Unlike the artists, who are well aware of the new pressures, the writers involved in the project have not discussed this, either in the workshops or in their anthology.[107] Although not describing them as 'dictatorships', in his introduction to the exhibition *After the Wall* (referring to the period 1989 to 1999), David Elliott mentioned that post-Communist art revolves around 'highly charged issues of economics, nationalism, religion, race, consumerism, poverty and alienation as well as around the impact of the newly privatized and "freed" mass media on social consciousness.'[108] Thus the fine arts have been concerned with new forms of constraints from the time of the opening of the Soviet bloc and have taken an openly critical stance towards old and new. Overt criticism of the newly experienced (re)forms is remarkable *per se*, since it indicates a changing consciousness; according to Louis Fürnberg's GDR song in the 1950s, the party is always right (*Die Partei, die Partei, die hat immer Recht*), and Stefan Wolle proposes that the person who doubts also accepts that the party could be wrong. With this confession, however, the socialist world would fall apart.[109] Self-criticism as such does not form part of the communist ideology and is alien to any dictatorial system; the hightened awareness and open expression of it is thus significant in itself and already marks transition.

Fig. 39

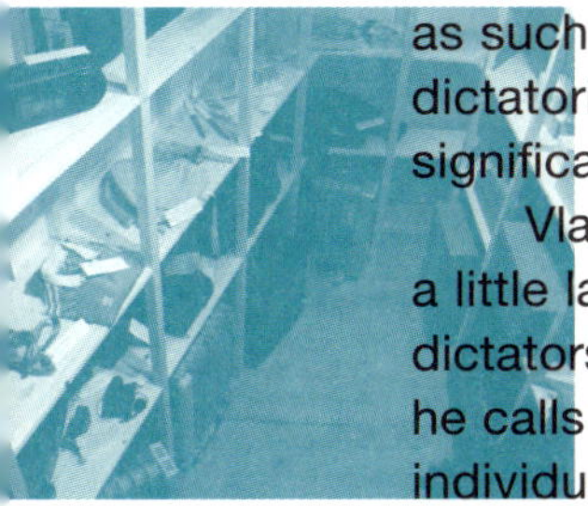

Vlad Nancă, in particular, mentioned that the EU project may have come a little late in the sense that people have already overcome the Communist dictatorships. For Nancă, the new problems to address now arise from what he calls 'turbo-capitalism.'[110] Wolle argues that after the opening of the wall individual East Germans may have still continued to dream of a democratic socialism and self-governance of the worker, most, however, did not want new social experiments, but the solid small (even petty) happiness associated with the average West German.[111] He concludes that the real divergence was towards a free market economy, free competition and a performance-oriented society, which explains the quick *Anschluss* to the FRG and unification of Germany within less than a year from the East German perspective. Nowhere is this better illustrated than in Peggy Meinfelder's installation *My First 100,- Westmark*, exhibited in 2004 [*Fig.* 39]. Her assemblage of items which East Germans bought with their first 100 (West) Deutsche Mark, received as a welcome present from West Germany after crossing the East-West borders, refers critically to the East being bought by the West, a form of economic colonialism on the basis of sheer consumerism.

Economic issues have become economic problems. Nancă even goes so far as describing financial restrictions as dictatorial.[112] Mirela Dauceanu, who, like Nancă, lives and works in Bucharest, produced *Daily Invalid Corruption* of 1995/2008, an installation originally exhibited in 1995, consisting of a recycled fridge, a TV and various bottles and boxes of pills [*Fig.* 40]. This work acknowledges the 1994 stabilization and economic growth in Romania as described by Gábor Hunya in an article published in *Post-Communist Economies*,[113] but criticizes it at the same time as being the result of corruption. In contrast to the other countries involved, in Romania the political party in power changed as a result of each of the general elections between 1992 and 2007, arguably causing major economic upheavals.

Fig. 40 *see pp. 56 f.*

Fig. 41

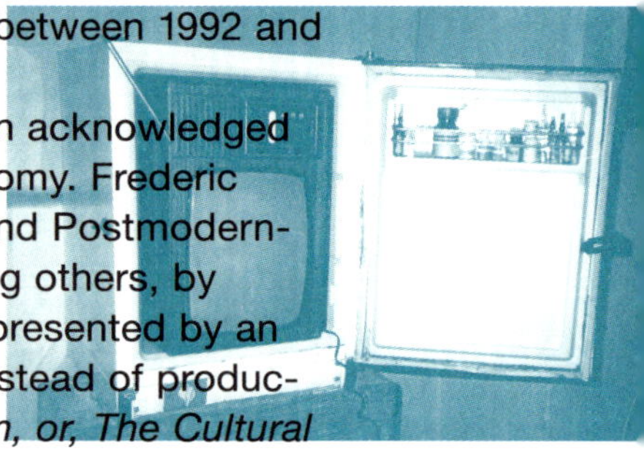

The influence of consumerism on culture has also been acknowledged in the West, which has a longer history of free market economy. Frederic Jameson in particular distinguished between Modernism and Postmodernism by correlating monopoly capitalism (represented, among others, by dictatorships) with the former and consumer capitalism (represented by an emphasis on marketing, selling, consuming commodities instead of producing them) with the latter in his seminal book *Postmodernism, or, The Cultural Logic of Late Capitalism*, which was based on an article of the same title published in 1984.[114] Jameson (from an American perspective) locates the former in the late nineteenth to the mid-twentieth centuries and the latter after that time. Accordingly, if Communist regimes are seen as a form of dictatorship, Postmodernism would begin in post-Communist countries after 1989. However, can such an equation be so easily made? Dauceanu's original installation of 1995 produced with material from Bucharest [*Fig.* 41] has been rebuilt with a second-hand refrigerator and television set found in Birmingham (UK) [*Fig.* 40]. As such, it questions such an equation, because despite similarities, the objects differ. Although Dauceanu has identified them as typical domestic consumer items of 1990s Romania, both have also been used in Pop Art in Britain; a television set is part of Richard Hamilton's seminal collage *Just What Is It That Makes Today's Homes So Different, So Appealing?* of 1956, albeit not as an installation, while Pop artist Clive Barber exhibited his *Fridge* at the Royal Academy Summer Exhibition in London in 2001 [*Fig.* 42]. In contrast, however, Dauceanu uses recycled objects. Suzana Milevska argues in her article 'The Readymade and the Question of the Fabrication of Objects and Subjects'[115] that East European installations and readymades arguably differ from those in Western cultures, because the 'quality of the manufactured objects was of secondary importance'[116] and thus the objects 'never look as perfect as the objects made in Western countries.'[117] Although the recycling aspect of the artist's work can be interpreted in various ways, it also demonstrates this difference between the objects of Pop Art and those used by Dauceanu and hence shows that Western Postmodernism cannot smoothly likened to developments in post-Communist countries.

Fig. 40 *see pp. 56 f.*

Fig. 42

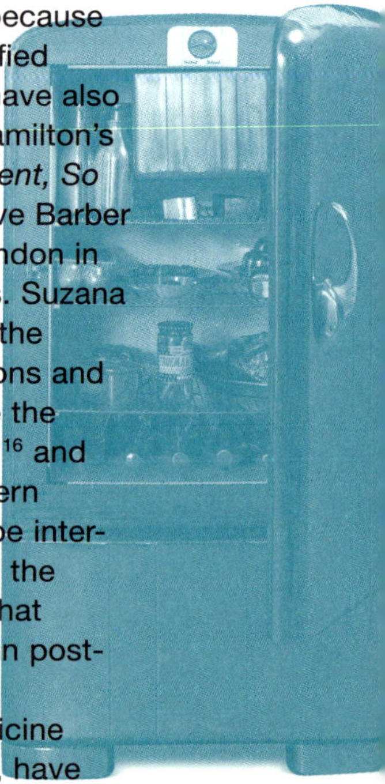

As a tribute to the project 'Overcoming Dictatorships', the medicine boxes, originally containing drugs only available in Romania [*Fig.* 43], have

Fig. 43

been ex-changed for boxes of paracetamol, the most common drug in Europe, bought in each of the countries participating in the project, so that despite containing the same drug, the boxes have text written in German, Italian, Polish, Czech, Hungarian and Romanian [*Fig.* 44]. As with Lodi's *Hanging History – Stock of History* [*Fig.* 33], the medical stock transcends the local without rendering it insignificant.

Fig. 44 *see page* 57
Fig. 33 *see page* 70
Fig. 30 *see pp.* 50 *f.*
Fig. 45 *see page* 49

Benýšek's *Prague Buffet* [*Fig.* 30] also refers to consumerism in the 1990s. It criticizes capitalism and the changes in values in the post-Communist Czech society. With *Midnight Watch* of 2007 [*Fig.* 45], an iconographic reference to Rembrandt's painting *Night Watch* of 1642, the artist goes a step further, depicting marginalization as one of the main negative outcomes of capitalism and consumerism:[118] Except for the smudged couple on the left who seem to have escaped, the people are depicted in derelict isolation. Alcohol, cigarettes and prostitution seem to have ruined their lives. So has advertising, which is condemned as blurring the real with the surreal: the artist has left open the question of whether the female figure behind the two men is a sales woman in a kiosk or part of an advertisement for sunglasses on a billboard. A fire-breathing animal in the front contributes to the surreality of the image. For the artist, capitalism and consumerism cause addiction and social isolation.

Figs. 46 *ff. see page* 79

Michele Zaggia's film, itself a mass medium of communication, entitled *Unpredicted Outcome* of 2007 [*Figs.* 46 *ff.*], addresses current dictatorships caused by communication technology. According to the artist, the increase in the role of the media, particularly television and the Internet, contributes to the globalized self-referentiality of signs – cultures interact not on the basis of real processes but on that of virtual realities, which are self-reproductions and predetermined by the media.[119] For him, globalization threatens to wipe out differences in culture, language, religion and ideologies. If this were to happen, it would give rise to a form of totalitarianism.[120]

Fig. 47 *see page* 79

The spiral, the corona of the eye at the beginning of the film [*Fig.* 47], stands for the charade of human belief in the ability to have direct and exhaustive knowledge of reality, despite realizing that knowledge is only mediated through reflection.[121] The reflection is part of the human condition, which is perpetually exposed to contingency, risk and the unforeseen, and thus split into fields like a board game, evoking a Snakes-and-Ladders world, which also signifies difference despite obvious similarities.[122] The wheel can be turned to the future, which is mainly seen in terms of technological advancement, but also the past, as it does in the film to the accelerating noise of train wheels. It is followed by a satire on totalitarian propaganda and its

Figs. 48 *and* 49
see page 79

promise to create a harmonious fable [*Figs.* 48 *and* 49], which is exposed, however, as grotesque through two accompanying male and female cartoon figures, which become a leitmotif of the film. Then the viewer is taken on a journey into the past: continuously changing portraits of major figures such as Joseph Stalin, but also Lech Walesa and Willy Brandt, and then signs of the twentieth and twenty-first centuries (including the swastika, hammer and

Figs. 50 *and* 51
see page 79

sickle, the symbol for dollars and the top of a Coca-Cola bottle; [*Figs.* 50 *and* 51] are shown to the sound of one of Hitler's speeches given in 1935, followed by Beethoven's *Ode to Joy*. No evaluating differentiation is made between political ideologies such as Communism, National Socialism, Stalinism, the Red Army Faction in Germany or Western democracy. In this respect, Zaggia's film is similar to the works produced by the Slovenian movement NSK (New Slovenian Art), which takes symbols and motifs from different totalitarian regimes and combines them with elements of both kitsch and classical avant-garde art.[123] Despite his own uniform approach to ideologies, Zaggia criticizes the way in which differences in language and music are levelled out (the spiral from the beginning of the film is shown again, but this time with English translations, to the music of American musicians Louis Prima and Herbie Hancock [*Fig.* 52]. He also condemns consumerism: instead of different faces representing different cultures, he leaves only the signs for dollars and euros on the black-and-white spiral following the one just mentioned [*Fig.* 53]. Like the previous spiral, it has an inner wheel, but this one has no lever of 'free will', which could influence the turning of the outer spiral. Hence, while Zaggia still hopes that the individual can turn the wheel as far as cultures are concerned, s/he has no free will in a solely consumer oriented society. In this respect, his outlook is gloomier than that of Göpfert who produced *Individuality Versus Dictatorship* [*Fig.* 28] and expressed his hope in one of the workshops that technology, political strategy, religion or any other ideology may never be allowed to have absolute control over human beings.[124] Göpfert puts his trust in the freedom of the individual; Zaggia questions it, and so does Benýšek, who sees capitalism and consumerism as causing addiction and isolation; and Nancă believes that financial restrictions form an overpowering authority. As with consumerism, but with more optimism, Zaggia is suspicious of globalization, while Dauceanu stresses the locally significant in a globalized market society in her 2008 installation *Daily Invalid Corruption*, thus finding an answer to Zaggia's literal question mark behind 'free will' in the spiral of his film. Both artists, however, see mass media as a danger threatening reality and truth.

Fig. 52 see page 79

Fig. 53 see page 79

Fig. 28 see pp. 58 f.

107 Kristina Kaiserová and Gert Röhrborn (eds.), *Present Tensions. European Writers on Overcoming Dictatorships*, Budapest, 2008. One of its contributors, Eduard Vacek, recognizes major problems with the new political powers, but would not call them dictatorships.

108 David Elliott, 'Introduction', 011.

109 See Hans-Hermann Hertle and Stefan Wolle, *Damals in der DDR*, 301.

110 See Vlad Nancă in Barbara Lubich, Workshop 2 in Wałbrzych (Poland).

111 See Hans-Hermann Hertle and Stefan Wolle, *Damals in der DDR*, 386f.

112 See Vlad Nancă in Barbara Lubich, Workshop 2 in Wałbrzych (Poland).

112 See Hans-Hermann Hertle and Stefan Wolle, *Damals in der DDR*, 3.

113 See Gábor Hunya, 'Romania 1990-2002: Stop-Go Transformation', *Post-Communist Economies*, vol. 10, June 1998, 241-258.

114 See Frederic Jameson, *Postmodernism, or, The Cultural Logic of Late Capitalism. Post-Contemporary Interventions*, Durham, NC, 1991 and *ibid.*, *New Left Review*, July-Aug. 1984, 52-92.

115 Translated and published in Laura Hoptman and Tomáš Pospiszyl (eds.), *Primary Documents*, 182-191.

116 *Ibid*, 182.

117 *Ibid*, 183.

118 See Zbyněk Benýšek below under 'In the Artists' Voices'.

119 Michele Zaggia, presentation of his work. See Barbara Lubich, Workshop 3 in Ústí nad Labem (Czech Republic).

120 See Michele Zaggia below under 'In the Artists' Voices'.

121 In Michele Zaggia, 'Maurizio Pellegrin', Alice Rubbini (ed.) *Writings on Maurizio Pellegrin. 1980-2006*, Milano, 2006, 144-147, 144, the artist argues that for him 'just as the human pretence to achieve absolute truth is madness, the conviction that there is no truth, that everything – as we say – is relative, is just as mad [...]. And instead there is truth, but truth, whose insuperable event is articulated in the infinite human practices under changeable meanings. Truth is then this; truth in the mode of philosophy, in the mode of science, in the mode of art.'

122 See Michele Zaggia in Barbara Lubich, Workshop 3 in Ústí nad Labem (Czech Republic).

123 For the movement, see Inke Arns, *Neue Slowenische Kunst (NSK) – eine Analyse ihrer künstlerischen Strategien im Kontext der 1980er Jahre in Jugoslawien*, exh. cat., Regensburg, Museum Ostdeutsche Galerie, 2002 and Marina Gržinić, 'Total Recall – Total Closure', Irwin (ed.), *East Art Map*, 321-331, 322f.

124 See Ulf Göpfert in Barbara Lubich, Workshop 3 in Ústí nad Labem (Czech Republic).

3 In a Changing Europe – Identities in Transition

Pavla Pecinkova notes in reference to Czech art in the 1990s that 'old certainties are no longer valid and new ones are not yet at hand.'[125] As the works and discussions in the workshops related to the project 'Overcoming Dictatorships' indicate, the in-between old and new still challenges the formation of identities, nurtured by the experiences gone through as citizens of countries which have become part of the EU but once belonged to the Soviet bloc, politically and economically dominated by the Soviet Union. The 'switch' from the bloc to the union has had major knock-on effects not only for its new members but also for the existing member states of the EU, and last but not least for the self-definition of Europe as an entity, as the following examples, catching only the tip of the iceberg, illustrate. A conservative encyclopedia published in (West) Germany in 1959 described Europe's history as encompassing Greco-Roman history, the Western (Roman) and Byzantine (Greek) Middle Ages, and the Modern Age until the two world wars (the latter being dominated by four main powers – France, Britain, Habsburg and Russia – from about 1700). The author added that even North America, and possibly to a lesser extent Latin America, can be seen as 'daughter cultures' of Europe.[126] A dictionary published after the reunification of Germany opens its entry on Europe with the following statement: 'Europe is a highly diverse western peninsula of Asia.'[127] These two descriptions, as has been argued, 'indicate the shift away from a hegemonic and triumphalist self-interpretation of Europe that saw itself as the centre of the world, with offshoots in the West without any connection with the East, to a description of itself as a marginal annex.'[128] Such an interpretation suits Susan Buck-Morss's critical response to Europe, when she proposes the 'bankruptcy of Western hegemony' due to 'ecological disasters' and 'fundamental structural contradictions between transnational global markets and Westphalian-based nation-states.'[129] The dictionary entry suggests a Chinese/Asian dominance, but here Buck-Moss has no replacement to offer because of an inherent problem: 'I do not think we can know, because our very conceptual frames for knowing are being drawn into the melting-down process, drawn into debris, and may themselves become part of the ruins.'[130]

Similar searches for new identities can be found in the art. In the latest *Oxford Companion to Western Art* published in 2001, Hugh Brigstocke defines the West as 'all cultures speaking a European language.'[131] Because they are historical centres of patronage, collecting markets and museums, he includes Spain, Italy, France, Germany, the UK and the USA, subsuming the rest as 'Central Europe' without any reference to 'East Europe' or further countries. Despite this introduction, the *Companion* has entries on all countries involved in the project 'Overcoming Dictatorships' except Romania, thus seemingly indicating an uncertainty about the boarders of Europe. However, how are Europe, the West, the East and the EU viewed by the artists involved in the project?

Fig. 54 see page 54

Zbigniew Czop's Poland as depicted in *Together – Separately* [*Fig.* 54] is not (yet) part of the EU. The etching plays with the historical bondage and the present difference through fantasy cityscapes of existing architectural landmarks – on the left are those to be found in EU countries, on the right are significant buildings situated in Poland. Similar to Silvestro Lodi's interpreta-

Fig. 33 see page 70

tion of the EU in *Hanging History – Stock of History* discussed above [*Fig.* 33], Poland remains separate, with a considerable gap between Europe and Poland and curiously only connected by the frame of the artist's etching, the sky with its dark and threatening clouds dramatically mixed with spells of sun and centrally bridged by an arch and a columned building similar to the Brandenburg Gate. A ring or 'lock' (as the artist interprets it) holds the two blocks and the two panels together.[132] Poland preserves its national and cultural identity, while it is only joined with the other part, Europe, via the gate and a ring/lock without a key, challenging European integration and decisional supranationalism.

Vlad Nancă also sees problems in European integration; compared with Czop's etching, however, the then 24-year-old Romanian expressed the uncertainty that many of the younger generation seem to face in *I Do Not*

Fig. 55 see page 74

Know What Union I Want to Belong to Anymore of 2003 [*Fig.* 55]. The idea for this work originates from a visit to a registry office in Bucharest in 2003.[133] In the wedding room, he saw the EU flag next to the Romanian one. Before 1989, the Soviet flag was always next to the Romanian flag. Although for him, it is a necessity for small countries in particular to become member states of the EU,[134] this work questions the function and relationships of national and European ideals, since the artist has exchanged the background colour of each flag, so that the hammer and sickle symbol of the Soviet flag (without the red star that appears in the upper canton) appears on the EU blue and the 12 stars on the Soviet red. The artist's reference to the Soviet flag being now 'exchanged' by that of the EU in the registry office hints at the parallels

Fig. 56

drawn between bloc and union, a union which seemingly raises suspicion.

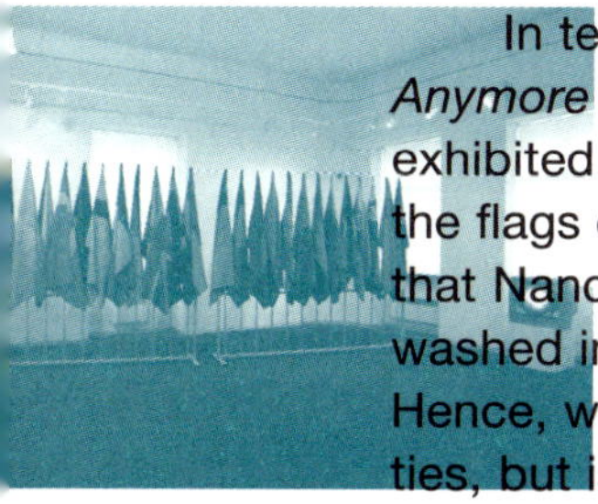

In terms of medium, *I Do Not Know What Union I Want to Belong to Anymore* is similar to *We Will Meet Again*, an installation by Jan Nálevka exhibited at the Futura Gallery in Prague in 2006 [*Fig.* 56]. Nálevka displayed the flags of the 26 countries belonging to the EU at the time. The difference is that Nancă's flags remain distinct from each other, but Nálevka's have been washed in a public laundrette until the colours have blended together. Hence, while similar in medium, *We will Meet Again* is not about uncertainties, but is rather, as Alberto Di Stefano argued, 'a strong visual metaphor of the melting pot awaiting us all'[135] and thus more similar to Michele Zaggia's *Unpredicted Outcome* as outlined below.

Nancă's other contribution is entitled *Ideal* and was produced as a result of the discussions related to the EU-funded project in 2007 [*Fig. 57*].[136] The Hungarian, German and Romanian flags all have a hole in the middle where emblems used to be during the Communist era (see p. 74). The Romanian coat of arms consisted of a scene depicting Romania's mineral wealth (an oil derrick, forests and mountains) basking in the glow of sun surrounded by sheaves of wheat wrapped with a ribbon in the national colours used on the flag between 1965 and 1989 [*Fig. 58*]. The red star at the top of the coat of arms symbolized Socialism and the words on the sheaves read Socialist Republic of Romania. The emblem of the GDR flag used between 1959 and 1990 consisted of a hammer and a compass surrounded by a ring of rye, representing the workers in the factory and the intelligentsia surrounded by the rye of the farmers [*Fig. 59*]. The Hungarian flag had the so-called Rákosi emblem between 1949 and 1956 named after Mátyás Rákosi, the *de facto* ruler of Communist Hungary during that time [*Fig. 60*]. Again there is the red star, the hammer and a rye stalk surrounded by rye as signifiers on the flag. Flags with a hole similar to those in Nancă's *Ideal* have been used in all three countries: anti-Soviet demonstrators cut out the Hungarian emblem during the Hungarian uprising in 1956; East Germans used the flag with the hole after the opening of the wall on 9 November 1989 up to German reunification on 3 October 1990; and anti-government protesters on the streets of Timişoara and Bucharest waved flags with a round hole in the middle during the week-long Romanian Revolution in late December 1989. The flags are displayed in chronological order, according to the artist. It does, however, also draw attention to issues related to the questionable central role played by Germany within the processes of the EU and its geographical 'relocation' into the heart of Europe after the opening of the East, problems not stressed by the artist, who emphasises rather the one hole which all three flags form when aligned, for him an 'ideal' scenario: 'By putting the three flags together I am aiming to realize a spiritual union that surpasses time, history and borders. The three countries (and their flags) are connected by the emptiness of the middle of the flag, a spiritual union of genuine revolutionary freedom, where no symbols spoil the essence of those days of liberty. It is an *Ideal* union I wish I could belong to.'[137] Despite the elevated mood and slightly sentimental nostalgia within the artist's self-reading, the iconoclastic and brutal act executed on the flags cannot disguise the void, a void that may also have been felt at the time the flags were used.

Not euros but dollars appear and American music is played in Zaggia's film *Unpredicted Outcome* of 2007 [*Figs. 46ff.*] as a symbol for the threat of wiping out differences through some forms of European integration.[138] As Bojana Pejić argues, the 'discourse about Europe has been dominated by metaphors which have featured the integration process as a journey, road or path leading "forwards", away from the "Europe of nation-states", towards a post-nationalist future in which peace, progress and prosperity would be

Fig. 57 see page 75

Fig. 58

Fig. 59

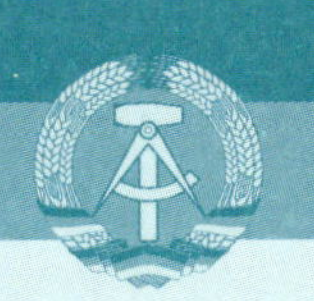

Fig. 60

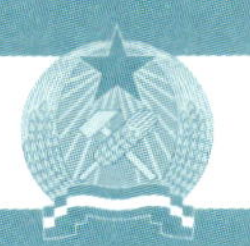

Figs. 46ff. see page 7

guaranteed by a more federal system of government.'[139] It is precisely this tension between protecting differences and finding a common ground in which communication (as regards economics as well as language, the latter being particularly important in view of the multi-lingual Europe) functions successfully that is at stake here and which the EU attempts to overcome by guaranteeing a federal system of government. Zaggia seems to be sceptical of those guarantees and portrays the journey as game and gambling in his film. The outcome, or rather the route, cannot be predicted: one may find on the way cultural, economic and electronic globalization (as portrayed by Zaggia's references to American music, dollars, euros and through the medium as such), disregarding diversity of any kind or nationalistic and religous fanaticism glorifying the self over the others (as Zaggia's portrait gallery of twentieth-century history reminds us of their realities in the past). One may also find those without 'free will', seduced citizens unable to act as self-directed individuals, and those who see in freedom enforcement rather than opportunity. The options for the formation of identities are varied, non-exclusive and non-essential in a Europe in flux which, because of the dramatic upheavals, opens up the need for (and chance of) repositioning.

[125]   See Pavla Pecinkova, *Contemporary Czech Painting*, 16f.

[126]   Th. Ohm, 'Europa. Allgemeine Geschichte', *Lexikon für Theologie und Kirche*, vol. 3, 1959, 1189-1194, 1189. For this example, see Lisa Kaul-Seidman, Jorgen S. Nielsen, Markus Vinzent, *European Identity and Cultural Pluralism*, Bad Homburg, 2003, 8.

[127]   S. Hradil, 'Europa', *Religion in Geschichte und Gegenwart*, vol. 2, 1999, 1661-1663, 1661.

[128]   Lisa Kaul-Seidman, Jorgen S. Nielsen, Markus Vinzent, *European Identity and Cultural Pluralism*, 8.

[129]   See Susan Buck-Morss, 'Theorizing Today: The Post-Soviet Condition', 26.

[130]   *Ibid.*

[131]   Hugh Brigstocke, 'Introduction', Hugh Brigstocke (ed.), *The Oxford Companion to Western Art*, Oxford, 2001, no page.

[132]   See Zbigniew Czop in Barbara Lubich, Workshop 2 in Wałbrzych (Poland).

[133]   See Vlad Nancă in Barbara Lubich, Workshop 3 in Ústí nad Labem (Czech Republic).

[134]   See *ibid.*

[135]   Alberto Di Stefano, 'Bohemia. A Desert Country Near the Sea', Suzanne Cotter, Andrew Nairne and Victoria Pomery (eds.), *Arrivals*, 108-110, 110.

[136]   See Vlad Nanc, Email to the author, 22 March 2008.

[137]   Vlad Nancă, below under 'In the Artists' Voices.'

[138]   See Michele Zaggia below under 'In the Artists' Voices'. One of the differences mentioned by Zaggia is language. He may agree in this respect with Steven Kellman who goes so far as to say that 'if identity is shaped by language [...], then monolingualism is a deficiency disorder' (cited after Roger Conover, 'Against Dictionaries: The East As She Is Spoke By the West', 349).

[139]   Bojana Pejić, Pejić, Bojana, 'The dialectics of normality', 022.

Art After Dictatorships

What is the role of art in post-dictatorial times or rather in processes of over-coming dictatorships? The question, raised at a symposium in Bucharest on 11 January 2007 for Romania, touches on a fundamental self-understanding of art and artists and their relationships with the political and social.[140] The remit of the inquiry certainly goes beyond Romania and other post-Com-munist countries; it has to be extended to any relationship between art and its socio-cultural impact: 'Can art ever take over the central point of power, being a symbol of openness and democracy?'[141] And if it could, should it take on this role? What are the ideological aspirations behind 'a central point of power', behind reflecting one of the grand narratives that seem to have been extinguished in 1989, when also elsewhere philosophers gave up looking for replacements? One might rather agree with Matthias Pauwels that 'every artistic act is itself already political'[142] or with Meta Haven's suggestion that 'art's political potency lies not so much in being "given" power, but in taking it.'[143] Art needs communicators and thus cannot create power itself, it will al-ways only mediate or represent. As it was 'able'[144] and therefore heavily used for mediating dictatorships, particularly through architecture, can art also mediate democracy, a democracy which some may call a reign of chaos and others a state of pluralism?[145]

The overturning of the Communist regimes, politico-symbolically related with the year 1989, has left its mark in visual and oral contributions made by those involved in the project 'Overcoming Dictatorships', perhaps more than in those works produced in the 1990s.

Remembering beyond mourning (nostalgia for the East) or simply re-cording historic moments can be found in Hauswald's installation *Time Travels* [*Fig.* 10]. He not only attempts to overcome collective identity formations of the past and celebrates the freedom, short-livedness and individualism of the West, but also critically engages with new collective identities, such as conformity of tourists, staged identities and the indifference caused by glob-alization. His photographs function as signifiers of dislocations and *attempts* at relocations. Each image depicting a specific location at a certain moment in time only seemingly *locates* it, because the very moment the picture is taken, this moment is gone – what remains, according to Jean Baudrillard, is a photograph as a medium of preservation of that particular locality.[146] In between creeps this 'slight time-lag which allows the image to exist before the world.'[147] This slight postponement, is the reason for the dislocation of any photograph; because of its obvious resemblance to what has been photo-graphed, 'the charm of the real,'[148] the viewer develops a desire for a reality

Fig. 10 *see pp.* 62 *f.*

Figs. 46*ff.*
see page 79

Figs. 33 *and* 35
see pp. 70 f.

Fig. 26 see page 77

Figs. 8 *and* 9
see page 80

Fig. 28 see pp. 58 f.

Fig. 46 ff. see page 79

Fig. 30 see pp. 50 f.

Fig. 40 see pp. 56 f.

Fig. 55 see page 74

Fig. 54 see page 54

Fig. 33 see page 70

Figs. 46 ff. see page 79

Fig. 40 see pp. 56 f.

Figs. 55 *and* 57
see pp. 74 f.

Fig. 31 see page 80

Fig. 10 see pp. 62 f.

Fig. 26 see page 77

Figs. 30 *and* 45
see pp. 49 f.

Fig. 28 see pp. 58 f.

Fig. 54 see page 54

Fig. 33 see page 70

that is gone, a desire which will remain an attempt to reach what can no longer, if ever, be reached. The same can be said for Zaggia's film *Unpredicted Outcome* [*Figs.* 46 *ff.*], although, compared with Hauswald, it shows less attempt to simulate reality. Art is mediating rather than 're-mediating', inventing rather than implementing, voicing unfulfilled desires and imagined threats. The over-coming of dictatorships may always remain an unfulfilled desire, a process – in process, a growing distancing from the experience through time and space at most.

Art after dictatorships is also alert to new dictatorships and the ways in which they can be avoided: through remembering as just mentioned, to which the works by Lodi [*Figs.* 33 and 35], Pinczehelyi [*Fig.* 26] and Zyśko [*Figs.* 8 and 9] also testify, and through an emphasis on individuality, as illustrated by Göpfert's *Individuality Versus Dictatorship* [*Fig.* 28] and Zaggia's *Unpredicted Outcome* [*Figs.* 46 *ff.*]. The latter also shows distrust of current systems that may have characteristics of dictatorships. The works of Benýšek, particularly *Prague Buffet* [*Fig.* 30], and Dauceanu's *Daily Invalid Corruption* [*Fig.* 40] approach critically the free market society; those of Nancă [*Fig.* 55] and Czop [*Fig.* 54], but also Lodi's *Hanging History – Stock of History* [*Fig.* 33] attempt to identify particularly the relationships between (their) countries and the EU, being critically aware and wary of the Communist bloc (and the) union. In other words, they attempt to overcome collective identity formations of the past (i.e. the Soviet bloc, National Socialism and Fascism), but also critically engage with the fear of new ones including consumerism, globalization and mass media. Their works not only question an assumed superiority of the West over the East, but challenge any compartmentalized thinking.

The works of Zaggia [*Figs.* 96 *ff.*] and Lodi [*Figs.* 33 and 35] suggest a more playful remembering and a questioning of current economies. This may also be argued for Dauceanu [*Fig.* 40] and Nancă [*Figs.* 55 and 57] and to some extent for Zyśko, particularly his *Obelisk* [*Fig.* 31]. Zaggia and Lodi experienced Fascism as a Second Generation, and the same goes for Nancă, Dauceanu and Zyśko, who are among the younger artists involved in the project, having experienced the years before 1989 only as children or young adults. Therefore, they belong, like Zaggia and Lodi in terms of Fascism, to a Second Generation of Communist societies. One may therefore argue for a generational gap signified by playfulness and engagement with the present in terms of material or subject (Lodi's dangling ties, Zaggia's comic figures, Dauceanu's criticism of consumerism, Nancă's questioning of identity and Zyśko's distrust of new dictatorships), while the past is felt more as a burden in Hauswald's *Time Travels* [*Fig.* 10], Pinczehelyi's *Almost 30 Years* [*Fig.* 26], Benýšek's paintings [*Figs.* 30 and 45], Czop's technique of etchings [*Figs.* 54 and 61] and Göpfert's tank [*Fig.* 28]. However, when one takes into account Czop's etching of *Together – Separately* [*Fig.* 54], questioning the relationship between the EU and her accession countries, and Göpfert's playful treatment of colour and design in *Individuality Versus Dictatorship* [*Fig.* 28] on the one hand (to name just a few) and the references to National Socialism and Fascism in Lodi's *Hanging History – Stock of History* [*Fig.* 33] and Zaggia's

Unpredicted Outcome [*Figs. 46 ff.*], and the use of the sickle and hammer
symbol by Nancă and Zyśko on the other (also just to name a few characteristics), such a generalizing interpretation becomes inaccurate, defying
the grand story of the generational gap, which, however, played a role in the
artists' discussions as mentioned in the introduction.[149]

Figs. 46 ff.
see page 73

Art works and artists brought together in this project and this book may
seem arbitrary and can certainly not be taken as representative of art after
dictatorships. The range of topics is too narrow, only scratching the surface
of contemporary art in Europe and involving but only a small and diverse
group of artists, some of whom do not even come from capital cities or
occupy well established places within the international art market. Aneta Szlak
would approve of this choice of artists, since she laments that one of the
two things that have not changed since Poland joined the EU, is that
'regardless of the importance of art scenes in different parts of the country,
international researchers rarely travel outside Warsaw.'[150] Creating 'post-
dictatorial art', however, would reinstate what the project itself tries to challenge, as if art could materialize what time and individuals have brought
down, a long and well-guarded wall and together with it a massive ideological narrative, to allow for attempting and approaching art as individuals in
democractic ways.

Hence, the project's emphasis has been dialogue and process, not
benchmarking and representation. Its has not been excavating the past for its
own sake, deepening the abyss between East and West, or turning East into
West, West into East, or mixing the two – it may be seen rather as overcoming what were given collective formations, especially including that of
East – and hence West – Europe. The term 'East Europe' itself brings to mind
Edward Said's deconstruction of 'isms'.[151] In his seminal book *Orientalism*
(first published in 1978), Said argues that the Orient (which comes from
the Latin *Oriens* for 'East') signifies a system of representations framed by
political forces that brought the Orient into Western consciousness. The
Orient as such exists only for the West and is constructed by and in relation to
the West. Although not all aspects of Said's Orientalism can be applied to
'East Europe', both terms have a reality through institutionalization.[152] Furthermore, there is the unconscious, untouchable certainty about what the
term is (Said calls it 'latent').[153] In the case of 'East Europe', this becomes
more and more problematic the longer the once defining 'Eastern bloc'
belongs to the past and new identities emerge.[154] As with 'the Orient', 'East
Europe' has been conceived as the opposite of the West, being separate
and backward-oriented.[155] Its regressive and superseded value(s) are judged
in terms of, and in comparison to, the progressing West, becoming the
distant Other.[156] As Boris Groys argues, even the East adopted such Western
expectations, 'confirming them by artificially simulating its cultural identity.'[157]

This project consciously included participants from Italy and Britain in
order to foster understanding between different regions and countries belonging to the EU. The main topic, 'Overcoming Dictatorships', did not want
to unite, adding another pillar to a proclaimed European cultural heritage,[158]

but rather to contribute to bridging the 'East' and the 'West', exposing the concepts of 'East' and 'West' Europe as in transition, which, as dominant cultural reference points for the contemporary visual, may also be on the way out, being replaced by an endless variety of issues, themes and positions.

140   Sarah James, 'Behind a Theoretical *Iron Curtain*', 10 convincingly argues that examining 'post-communist artistic production allows us to deepen our understanding' of exactly this relationship.

141   Meta Haven, n.t., *Regimes of Representation. Art & Politics Beyond the House of People*, pamphlet published on the occasion of the symposium Regimes of Representation. Art and Politics Beyond the House of People, Bucharest, 11 Jan. 2007. The conference was a follow-up of The Museum of Conflict. Art as Political Strategy in Post-Communist Europe, conference, Maastricht, 11 Sept. 2006 (see www.museumofconflict.eu).

142   Matthias Pauwels, moderating The Museum of Conflict.

143   See Meta Haven, Imagination of Engagement, paper given at The Museum of Conflict.

144   Boris Groys attempts to explain the ability of art by arguing that an 'artist operates on the same territory as ideology' and thus art is 'much more powerfully and productively in the context of politics than in the context of the market' (Boris Groys, *Art Power*, Cambridge/Massachusetts and London/GB, 2008, 8).

145   See Eleanor Heartney, *Art & Today*, London, 2008, 8.

146   See Jean Baudrillard, *The Perfect Crime*, London, 1996, 88.

147   *Ibid.* Baudrillard adds that this does not apply to a 'computer-generated image', in fact any digital image.

148   *Ibid.*

149   See above.

150   Aneta Szlak, 'The Uncertain Condition', Suzanne Cotter, Andrew Nairne and Victoria Pomery (eds.), *Arrivals*, 30f., 30. The other thing that has not changed is the demand to define 'Polishness.'

151   Although not referring directly to Said and also with a slightly different conclusion, Bojana Pejić holds a similar view in her essay 'The dialectics of normality', 016-028. She argues that there are only two positions on the topic, that from within the East and that from the outside (see *ibid*, 018). Although arguably there are more than just these two perspectives, in the context here, her perspective is complementary to mine, since she 'acts from within' (*ibid.*), while I am positioned, to use her words, on the 'outside.' See also the following literature, although the authors do not refer to art in particular: Bo Stråth, 'Multiple Europes: Integration, Identity and Demarcation to the Other', Bo Stråth (ed.), *Europe and the Other and Europe as the Other*, Brussels, 2000, 385-420; Maria Todorova,

Inventing the Balkans, Oxford, 1997 and Holm Sundhaussen, 'Der Balkan: Ein Plädoyer für Differenz', *Geschichte und Gesellschaft*, vol. 29, 2003, 608-624.

152   See above.

153   See Edward W. Said, *Orientalism. Western Conceptions of the Orient*, London, 1995 (first published in 1978), 201.

154   See, for example, Bojana Pejić's 1999 comment about her puzzled search 'during the past years to detect what is *typically Western* in the art of the East which has been made *after* the Wall'. See Bojana Pejić, 'The dialectics of normality', 018. Susan Buck-Morss argues that the 'era of Western hegemony' lasted from 1492 to 1992, and thus is already over ('Theorizing Today: The Post-Soviet Condition', 25).

155   According to Bojana Pejić, 'The dialectics of normality', 025, Tony Blair called the Balkans during the Kosovo War 'Europe's backyard'.

156   See, for example, Aneta Szlak, 'The Uncertain Condition', 30, who claims that for 'a long time, international contacts [with Poland] were characterised by certain modes of operation, often swinging between them: mimicry ("we are exactly the same as you"); playfully exotic ("we are so wild and different") and the modest apprentice ("please teach me, I want to be like you").' See also Bojana Pejić, 'The dialectics of nor-mality', who critically refers to the exotic and the suspicious need not to construct a 'new cabinet of (eastern) curiosities' (018; see also 024). Consequently, Pejić also argues for a state of normality and self-critically questions the inclusion of only Eastern artists in their exhibition (see 019).

157   See Boris Groys, *Art Power*, 157. See also Petr Vaňous, 'The Continuity of Painting (Clearly) Exits', *Nová trpělivost*, exh. cat., Prague, Exhibition Hall Mánes, 2007, 669f., 69, who writes about art in the Czech Republic that 'during the first half of the 1990s [...] newly defined official art [...] naturally looked for its models in the cultural centres of the USA and Western Europe.'

158   See, for example, Hans-Gert Poettering, Priority is Dialogue for Partnership and Tolerance (inaugural speech by the new president of the European Parliament), 13 Feb. 2007 (see www.youtube.com), who mentions the suffering of two world wars, the achievements of Liberalism in the nineteenth century and the Age of Enlightenment as such pillars.

Bibliography
Sources
Secondary literature

Bibliography

Except for the unpublished material related to the project directly (e.g. questionnaires and workshop discussions), writing by and on the artists (including monographs and exhibition catalogues) is listed under the bibliography to each artist (see 'Biographies of the Artists').

Sources

A

Adorno, Theodor *(et al.), Aesthetics and Politics,* London and New York, 2007

B

Baudrillard, Jean, *The Perfect Crime,* London, 1996
Bishop, Claire, *Participation. Documents of Contemporary Art,* London and Cambridge, 2006
Brigstocke, Hugh, 'Introduction', Hugh Brigstocke (ed.), *The Oxford Companion to Western Art,* Oxford, 2001, no page

G

Göpfert, Ulf, Questionnaire (Answer to the question: What does 'overcoming dictatorships' mean to you?), April 2007, unpublished (archive material of the project, TU Dresden)

H

Hradil, S., 'Europa', *Religion in Geschichte und Gegenwart,* vol. 2, 1999, 1661-1663
The Museum of Conflict. Art as Political Strategy in Post-Communist Europe, conference, Maastricht, 11 Sept. 2006 (www.museumofconflict.eu)
Hein, Christoph, *Die Ritter der Tafelrunde und andere Stücke,* Berlin, 1990
Hoptman, Laura and Pospiszyl, Tomáš (eds.), *Primary Documents. A Sourcebook for Eastern and Central European Art since the 1950s,* Cambridge/Mass., 2002
The Institute, pamphlet of the Institute for the Investigation of Communist Crimes in Romania, n.d. (published by the Institute)

J

Jameson, Frederic, *Postmodernism, or, The Cultural Logic of Late Capitalism. Post-Contemporary Interventions,* Durham, NC, 1991
Jameson, Frederic, 'Postmodernism, or, The Cultural Logic of Late Capitalism. Post-Contemporary Interventions', *New Left Review,* July-Aug., 1984, 52-92

K

Kaiserová, Kristina and Röhrborn, Gert (eds.), *Present Tensions. European Writers on Overcoming Dictatorships,* Budapest, 2008
Lodi, Silvestro, Questionnaire (Answer to the question: What does 'overcoming dictatorships' mean to you?), April 2007, unpublished (archive material of the project, TU Dresden)
Lubich, Barbara, Workshop 2 in Wałbrzych (Poland), 30 March to 1 April 2007, DVD, unpublished (archive material of the project, TU Dresden)
Lubich, Barbara, Workshop 3 in Ústí nad Labem (Czech Republic), 17 to 19 May 2007, DVD, unpublished (archive material of the project, TU Dresden)
Lubich, Barbara, Workshop 4 in Budapest (Hungary), 12 to 14 Oct. 2007, DVD, unpublished (archive material of the project, TU Dresden)
Lubich, Barbara, Workshop 5 in Bucharest (Romania), 7 to 9 Dec. 2007, DVD, unpublished (archive material of the project, TU Dresden)
Lubich, Barbara, Workshop 6 in Trent (Italy), 9 to 10 May 2008 DVD, unpublished (archive material of the project, TU Dresden)

M

Michnik, Adam, *Die Kirche und die polnische Linke. Von der Konfrontation zum Dialog,* Munich, 1980
Müller, Heiner, *Was von den Träumen blieb. Eine Bilanz der sozialistischen Utopie,* Berlin, 1993

O

Ohm, Th., 'Europa. Allgemeine Geschichte', *Lexikon für Theologie und Kirche,* vol. 3, 1959, 1189-1194
Oprea, Marius, quoted in *The Institute,* pamphlet of the Institute for the Investigation of Communist Crimes in Romania, n.d. (published by the Institute)

P

Poettering, Hans-Gert, Priority is Dialogue for Partnership and Tolerance (inaugural speech by the new president of the European Parliament), 13 Feb. 2007 (see http://www.youtube.com)
Postman, Neil, *The Disappearance of Childhood,* New York, 1982

R

Rancière, Jacques, *The Politics of Aesthetics,* London and New York, 2008 (2004)

S

Sariban, Alla, *Verinnerlichung der Diktatur. Ein Briefwechsel in Zeiten der Transformation,* Dienheim, 2007
Said, Edward W., *Orientalism. Western Conceptions of the Orient,* London, 1995 (first published in 1978)
Scherzer, Landolf, *Der Erste,* Rudolstadt, 1988
Schmitt, Carl, *Die Diktatur. Von den Anfängen des modernen Souveränitätsgedankens bis zum proletarischen Klassenkampf,* Berlin, 2006 (first edition in 1921)
Walser, Martin, *Deutsche Sorgen,* Frankfurt, 1997
Wolf, Christa, *Was bleibt,* Berlin, 1990

Z

Zaggia, Michele, Questionnaire (Answer to the question: What does 'overcoming dictatorships' mean to you?), April 2007, unpublished (archive material of the project, TU Dresden)

Secondary literature

A

Akademie der Künste (ed.), *Denkmale und kulturelles Gedächtnis nach dem Ende der Ost-West-Konfrontation,* Berlin, 2000
Andrási, Gábor, 'The Seventies', Gábor Andrási, Gábor Pataki, György Szücs, András Zwickl (eds.), *The History of Hungarian Art in the Twentieth Century,* 181-209
Andrási, Gábor and Zwickl, András, 'Contemporary Art in the Ninetees', Gábor Andrási, Gábor Pataki, György Szücs and András Zwickl (eds.), *The History of Hungarian Art in the Twentieth Century,* 249-267
Andrási, Gábor, Pataki, Gábor, Szücs, György and Zwickl, András (eds.), *The History of Hungarian Art in the Twentieth Century,* Budapest, 1999
Arns, Inke, *Neue Slowenische Kunst (NSK) – eine Analyse ihrer künstlerischen Strategien im Kontext der 1980er Jahre in Jugoslawien,* exh. cat., Regensburg, Museum Ostdeutsche Galerie, 2002

B

Besier, Gerhard, 'Einleitung', *Kirchliche Zeitgeschichte/Contemporary Church History,* vol. 20, 2007, 288-297 and 217-223
Besier, Gerhard, *Das Europa der Diktaturen. Eine neue Geschichte des 20. Jahrhunderts,* Munich, 2006
Biemann, Ursula, 'Preface', Anselm Franke (ed.), *B-Zone,* 4f.
Bobbio, Norberto, *Democracy and Dictatorship. The Nature and Limits of State Power,* Oxford, 1989
Buck-Morss, Susan, 'Theorizing Today: The Post-Soviet Condition', *Log,* winter issue, 2008, 23-31

Burgdorf, Wolfgang, *'Chimäre Europa': Antieuropäische Diskurse in Deutschland (1648-1999),* Bochum, 1999

C

Carrier, James (ed.), *Occidentalism. Images of the West,* Oxford, 1995
Císař, Karel, 'Toward "Minor" Art', Suzanne Cotter, Andrew Nairne and Victoria Pomery (eds.), *Arrivals,* 106f.
Conover, Roger, 'Against Dictionaries: The East As She Is Spoke By the West', Irwin (ed.), *East Art Map,* 349-361
Cotton, Charlotte, *The Photograph as Contemporary Art,* London, 2004
Cotter, Suzanne, Nairne, Andrew and Pomery, Victoria (eds.), *Arrivals>Art from the New Europe,* exh. cat., Oxford, Modern Art Oxford and Turner Contemporary, 2007

D

Dietrich, Ute and Winkler, Martina (eds.), *Okzidentbilder. Konstruktionen und Wahrnehmungen,* Leipzig, 2000
Drury, Richard, Machalický, Jiří and Vaňous, Petr (eds.), *Typický Obraz,* exh. cat., Prague, Galerie Nová síň, 2007

E

Elkins, James, *Stories of Art,* New York and London, 2002
Elliott, David, 'Introduction', Bojana Pejić and David Elliott (eds.), *After the Wall,* 011
Elliott, David and Tazzi, Pier Luigi (eds.), *Wounds: Between Democracy and Redemption in Contemporary Art,* exh. cat., Stockholm, Moderna Museet, 1998
Erjavec, Ales (ed.), *Postmodernism and the Postsocialist Condition,* Berkeley, 2003

F

Féhér, Ferenc *et al.* (eds.), *Dictatorship Over Needs,* Oxford, 1983
Fowkes, Maja and Reuben (eds.), *Revolution Is Not a Garden Party,* Manchester, 2007
Franke, Anselm (ed.), *B-Zone. Becoming Europe and Beyond,* Berlin and Barcelona, 2006
Franke, Anselm, 'Introduction', Anselm Franke (ed.), *B-Zone,* 6-15
Fulbrook, Mary, *The Anatomy of a Dictatorship. Inside the GDR, 1949-1989,* New York and Oxford, 1995

G

Gehler, Michael, *Europa,* Frankfurt/M., 2002
Groys, Boris, *Art Power,* Cambridge/Massachusetts and London/GB, 2008
Gržinić, Marina, 'On the Re-

Politicisation of Art Through Contamination', Irwin (ed.), *East Art Map,* 477-486
Gržinić, Marina, 'Total Recall – Total Closure', Irwin (ed.), *East Art Map,* 321-331

H

Haven, Meta, n.t., *Regimes of Representation. Art & Politics Beyond the House of People,* pamphlet published on the occasion of the symposium Regimes of Representation. Art and Politics Beyond the House of People, Bucharest, 11 Jan. 2007 (copy from the MNAC, Bucharest)
Hartewig, Karin and Lüdtke, Alf (eds.), *Die DDR im Bild. Zum Gebrauch der Fotografie im anderen deutschen Staat,* Göttingen, 2004
Hauer, Armin, *Kunst in der DDR,* exh. cat., Berlin, Nationalgalerie, 2003
Heartney, Eleanor, *Art & Today,* London, 2008
Hellwig-Schmid, Regina (ed.), *Donumenta. Ars Danubiana,* exh. cat., Regensburg, 2007
Hertle, Hans-Hermann and Wolle, Stefan, *Damals in der DDR. Der Alltag im Arbeiter- und Bauernstaat,* Munich, 2006
Hoffmann, Detlev, 'Was bezeugt der Augenzeuge? Auch ein Versuch, die Arbeitsweisen der Geschichte und der Kunstgeschichte als sinnvoll im Umgang mit der Fotografie zu beschreiben', Anton Holzer and Timm Starl (eds.), *Fotografie/Geschichte. 25 Jahre Fotogeschichte,* Marburg 2005, 25-28
Homburg, Cornelia, *German Art Now,* London and New York, 2004
Hoptman, Laura and Pospiszyl, Tomáš, 'Introduction', *Primary Documents,* 9-11
Hunya, Gábor, 'Romania 1990-2002: Stop-Go Transformation', *Post-Communist Economies,* vol. 10, June 1998, 241-258

I

Irwin (ed.), *East Art Map. Contemporary Art and Eastern Europe,* London, 2006

J

James, Sarah, 'Behind a Theoretical Iron Curtain', *Art Monthly,* June 2008, 7-10
Jarausch, Konrad H. (ed.), *Dictatorship As Experience. Towards a Social-Cultural History of the GDR,* New York et al., 1999

K

Kaul-Seidman, Lisa, Nielsen, Jorgen S., Vinzent, Markus, *European Identity and Cultural Pluralism,* Bad

Homburg, 2003
Kiss Gy, Csaba, 'Central European Myths of Conquest', *Minorities Research,* no. 1, 1999 (http://epa.oszk.hu/html/vgi/boritolapuj.phtml?id=463)
Klein, Naomi, *No-Logo: No Space, No Choice, No Jobs,* London, 2001
Klotz, Katharina, 'Foto – Montage – Plakat. Zur politischen Ikonographie der "sozialistischen Sichtagitation" in der frühen DDR', Karin Hartewig and Alf Lüdtke (eds.), *Die DDR im Bild,* 29-49
Kolinsky, Eva and Nickel, Hildegard Maria (eds.), *Reinventing Gender. Women in Eastern Germany Since Unification,* London, 2003
Koralova, Ilina, 'Introduction', Ilina Koralova (ed.), *Against. Within,* 7-9
Koralova, Ilina (ed.), *Against. Within,* Graz, 2006
Kříž, Jan (ed.), *Dva konce století. The End of Two Centuries,* exh. cat., české museum výtvarných umění, 2000
Kunstforum Ostdeutsche Galerie Regensburg (ed.), *Crossing Frontiers. Határátl Épések. Grenzgänger,* exh. cat., Regensburg, Kunstforum Ostdeutsche Galerie, 2006 and Budapest, Museum of Contemporary Art/Ludwig Museum, 2007

L

Ladd, Brian, 'East Berlin Political Monuments in the Late German Democratic Republic. Finding a Place for Marx and Engels', *Journal of Contemporary History,* no. 1, 2002, 91-104
Lindner, Bernd, 'Ein Land – zwei Bilderwelten. Fotografie und Öffentlichkeit in der DDR', Karin Hartewig and Alf Lüdtke (eds.), *Die DDR im Bild,* 189-206

M

McFaul, Michael, *Between Dictatorship and Democracy. Russian Post-Communist Political Reform,* Washington, 2004
Močnik, Rastko, 'EAST!', Irwin (ed.), *East Art Map,* 343-348

O

Oroveanu, Mihai (ed.), *MNAC,* Bucharest, 2004

P

Pecinkova, Pavla, *Contemporary Czech Painting,* East Roseville, 1993
Palin, Michael, *New Europe,* London, 2007
Pejić, Bojana a avid (eds.), *After the Wall. Art and Culture in Post-Communist Europe,* exh. cat., Stockholm, Moderna Museet, 1999 and Budapest, Ludwig-Museum of

Contemporary Art, 2000
Pejić, Bojana, 'The dialectics of normality', Bojana Pejić and David Elliott (eds.), *After the Wall,* 016-028
Plessen, Marie-Louise von (ed.), *Idee Europa. Entwürfe zum Ewigen Frieden. Ordnungen und Utopien für die Gestaltung Europas von der pax romana zur Europäischen Union. Eine Ausstellung als historische Topographie,* Berlin, 2003
Pospiszyl, Tomás 'Jakub Hošek', Suzanne Cotter, Andrew Nairne and Victoria Pomery (eds.), *Arrivals,* 96

R
Radomska, Magdalena, 'Semantyczne pole minowe', *Art. Magazyn o sztuce,* no. 4, 2007, 22-25
Rehberg, Karl-Siegbert, Ideenkunst als Schlüssel der Gesellschaftsanalyse. Der Fall der DDR, conference paper, Overcoming Dictatorships. Intellettuali e Regimi, as part of the Workshop 6 in Trent (Italy), 9-10 May 2008
Rétlhy, Ákos (ed.), *Statue Park. Gigantic Monuments from the Age of Communist Dictatorship,* Budapest, no date (see also website: szoborpark.hu)

S
Sabrow, Martin (ed.), *Wohin treibt die DDR-Erinnerung? Dokumentation einer Debatte*, Göttingen, 2007
Sauerland, Karol, 'Die Rolle der katholischen Kirche Polens', *Kirchliche Zeitgeschichte/Contemporary Church History,* vol. 2, 2007, 288-297
Stefano, Alberto Di, 'Bohemia. A Desert Country Near the Sea', Suzanne Cotter, Andrew Nairne and Victoria Pomery (eds.), *Arrivals*, 108-110
Stråth, Bo, 'Multiple Europes: Integration, Identity and Demarcation to the Other', Bo Stråth (ed.), *Europe and the Other and Europe as the Other,* Brussels, 2000, 385-420
Sundhaussen, Holm, 'Der Balkan: Ein Plädoyer für Differenz', *Geschichte und Gesellschaft,* vol. 29, 2003, 608-624
Szlak, Aneta, 'The Uncertain Condition', Suzanne Cotter, Andrew Nairne and Victoria Pomery (eds.), *Arrivals,* 30f.

T
Tighe, Carl, *The Politics of Literature. Poland 1945-1989,* Cardiff, 1999
Todorova, Maria, *Inventing the Balkans,* Oxford, 1997

V
Vaňous, Petr, 'The Continuity of Painting (Clearly) Exits', *Nová*

trpělivost, exh. cat., Prague, Exhibition Hall Mánes, 2007, 669f.
Vinzent, Jutta, *Identity and Image. Refugee Artists from Nazi Germany in Britain, 1933-1945,* Kromsdorf/Weimar, 2006

W
Weszkalnys, Gisa, 'The Disintegration of a Socialist Exemplar: Discourses on Urban Disorder in Alexanderplatz, Berlin', *Space & Culture,* no. 10, 2007, 207-230
Weizman, Ines, 'Critique Without Memory, or Memory Without Critique', Ilina Koralova (ed.), *Against. Within,* 21-35

Appendices

I
In the Artists' Voices

What does 'overcoming dictatorships' mean in the words of the artists?
Writing on art, particularly since the Barthesian proclamation of the death of
the author and the replacement of the author with the Foucauldian 'author –
function', may lead to silencing the artist, running the risk of objectifying
not only the art work but also its maker.[159] To counteract this, and also in line
with the project 'Overcoming Dictatorships' which consisted of verbal
encounter in both real and electronic space, the illustrations of the artists'
works executed around the topic are accompanied by statements in which the
artists explore their works and outline their views on how to overcome
dictatorships.

Jutta Vinzent

[159] See also Bojana Pejić, 'The dialectics of normality', who
refers to Linda Alcoff's article 'The Problem of Speaking
for Others'. Pejić argues that the author participates
in the construction of the artists' subject-positions (016).

Saint Sebastian, 1997 [*Fig.* 7]

The darkest picture of the triptych is *Saint Sebastian* of 1997. There is
an inquisitorial committee working in the background. It is there to
question an endless line of wretches with the help of rheostats or com-
puters. The content is eternal (perpetual), hence the reference to
Christian iconography – only the context and the methods are changing.

Prague Buffet, 1995 [*Fig.* 30]

This painting was created in the mid-1990s. It tells stories. We find our-
selves in a small restaurant, in which people sit in groups and talk.
But there are two more events. In the middle of the picture is a vulture-
like bird preparing to catch a vainly escaping songbird. Pasolini's film
about the crucifixion of Christ runs on a TV depicted below the hunted
bird. The moment when Christ shouts his last words is frozen on the
screen. Seemingly paradoxically, nobody in the room watches the
cruel hunting scene or the crucifixion of Christ. This represents to me
the atmosphere of the society in the mid-1990s, when people were not
interested in any topic beyond consumerism and their daily concerns,
neither in spirituality – here symbolised by the crucifixion – nor in the
practices of predators scrambling mercilessly for their prey as shown in
the bird hunt.

Midnight Watch, 2007 [*Fig.* 45]

This is the central picture of the triptych. While *Saint Sebastian* refers
to Communist Czechoslovakia, *Prague Buffet* reflects on post-Communist 'Wild Capitalism' and challenging values. *Midnight Watch* is a pro-
found transcription of the contemporary situation as a logical outcome
of the previous periods.

2007

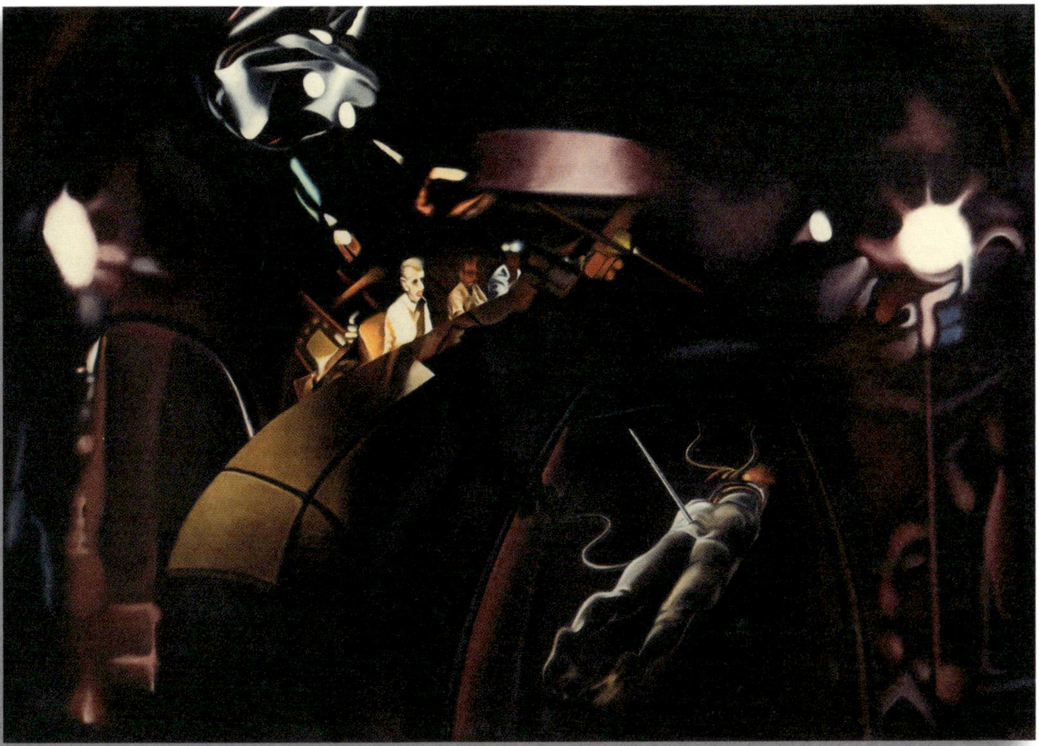

  Saint Sebastian, 1993
Midnight Watch, 2007

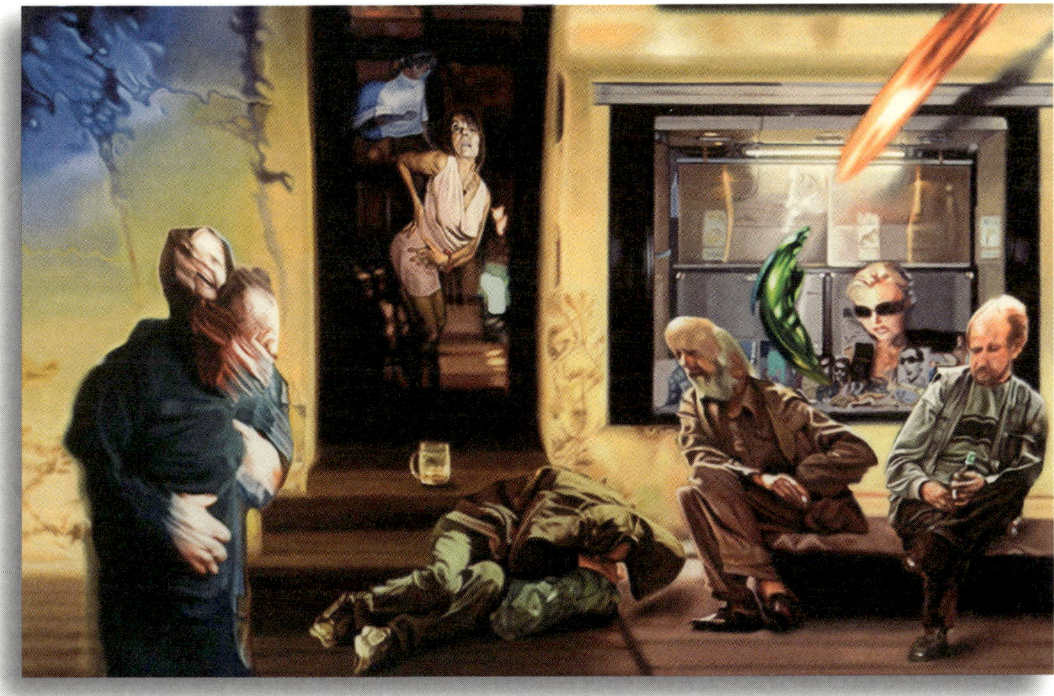

Fig. 7

Fig. 45

   Zbyněk Benýšek, Prague Buffet, 1995

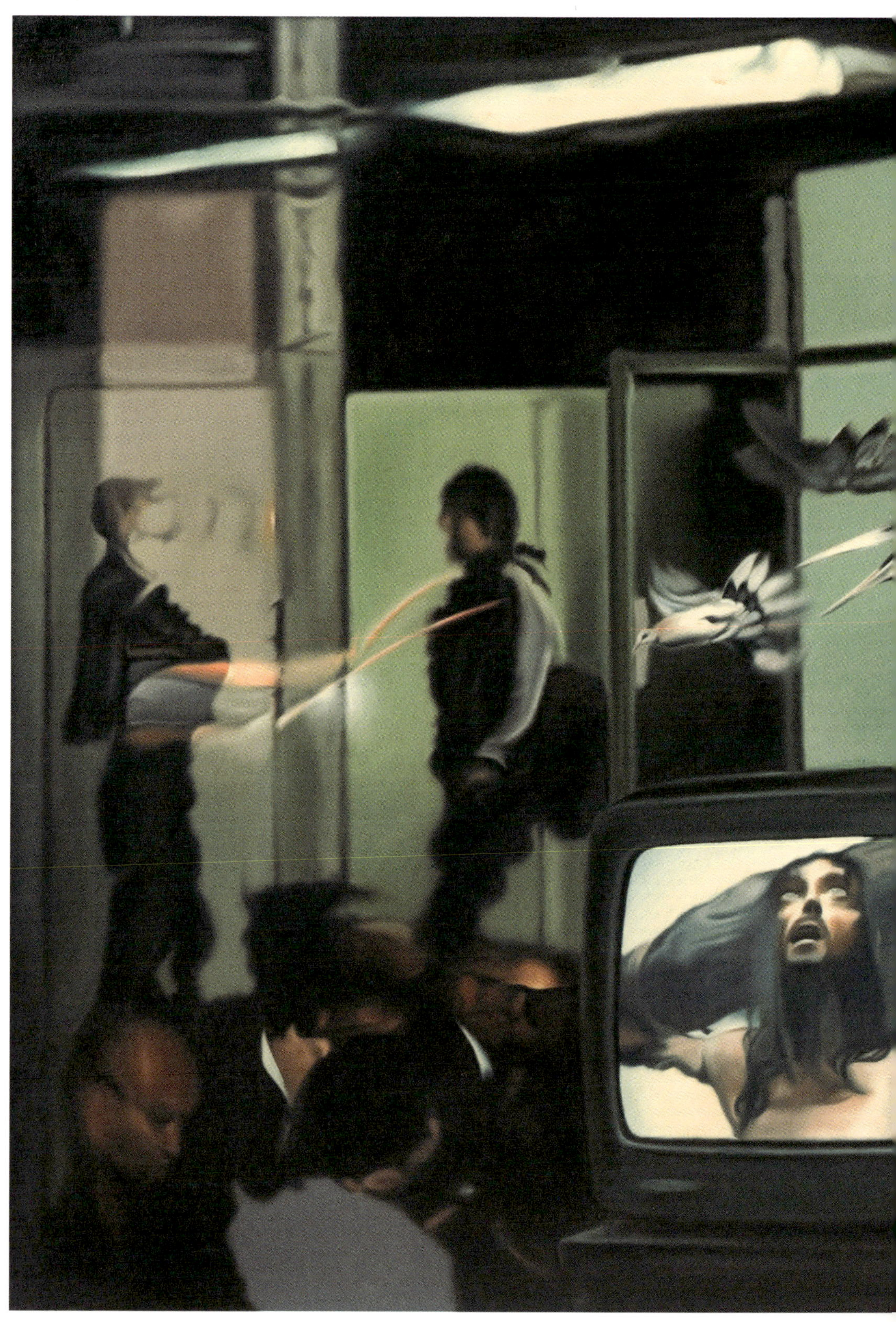

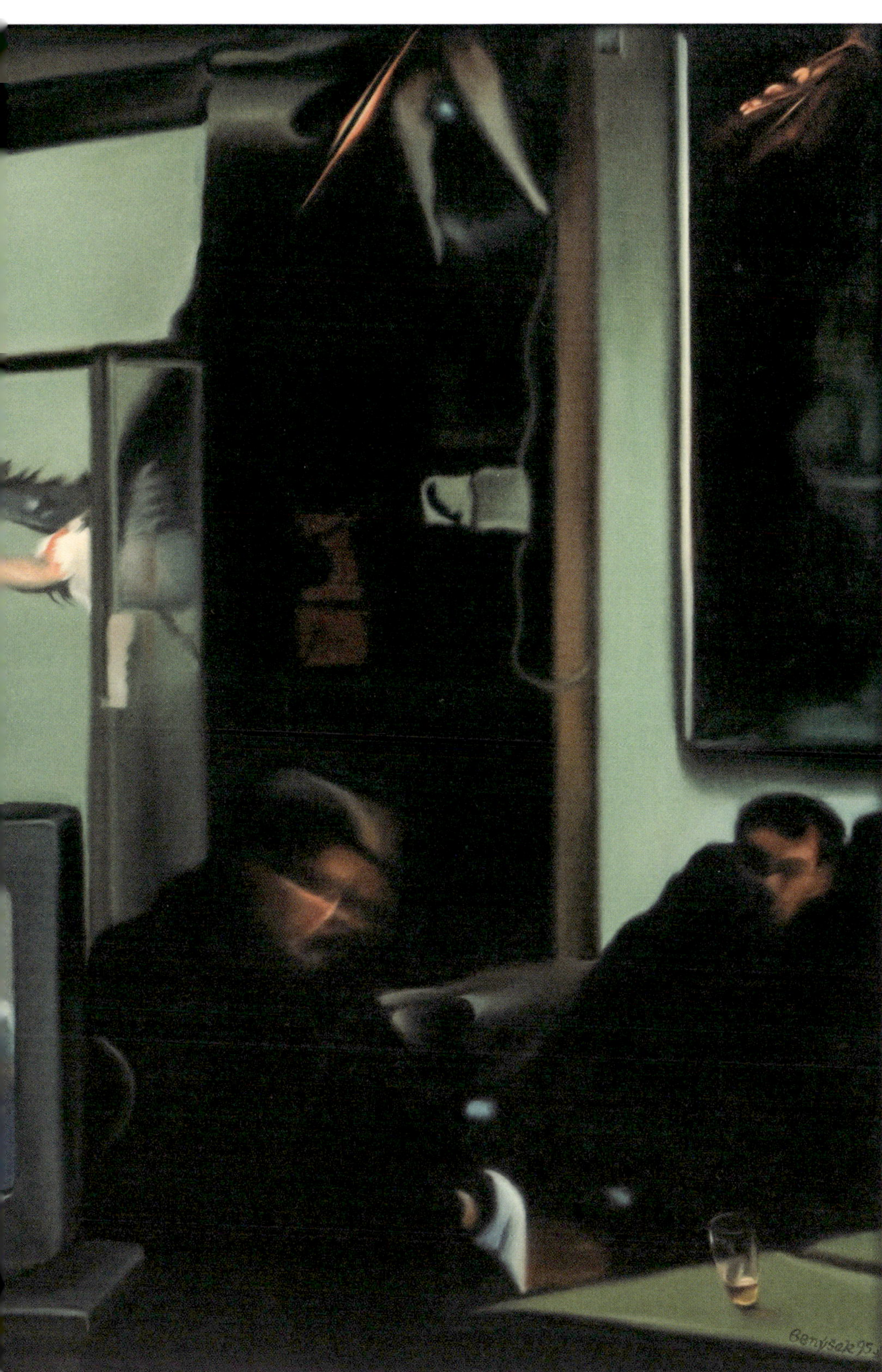

In the 1970s a book entitled *The Dialogues* was published in Poland. The author of this book, Stanisław Lem, was a distinguished and erudite philosopher and visionary. In his book he discussed, among other things, the secrets of a State in a totalitarian system. Lem said that the 'secret causes damage to someone for the sake of the inviolability of the system.' It is a kind of dialogue about social existence and the tragic aspects of various instruments of pressure and their effect. This dialogue is set in the ancient orchard of Academos, and maybe this location protected it from being censored. Totalitarian ideology embraces people fixed in unvarying places, where societies are made up of a mass without reflection, a mass which needs leaders who present aims to conform to their deviation (see *Awful Pedagogy* of 1986; *Fig.*61). These leaders use means of direct pressure and repression to silence disloyal people, whom they call enemies of the State.

The eruption of resistance meant that police and government could not suppress opposition, which was related to living conditions and was emphasized by intellectuals. As a result the political system collapsed, and the time came to take a deep breath and create hope to be oneself.

Since then we have got up from our knees, and are building a society on the basis of hope and normality. With time the need to be together blurs the historical and cultural differences. Meeting people from other cultures is an educational necessity in uniting Europe and the world (*Together – Separately*, undated; *Fig.*54). We see here and there almost the same needs. But suddenly and unnoticeably there arises new social needs – consumption, a new ideology. This social element is created by another totalitarianism – advertising – its tools are based on psychological manipulation. It is not primitive but subtle, and it creates the necessity of possession. We must change values in our defence.

2007

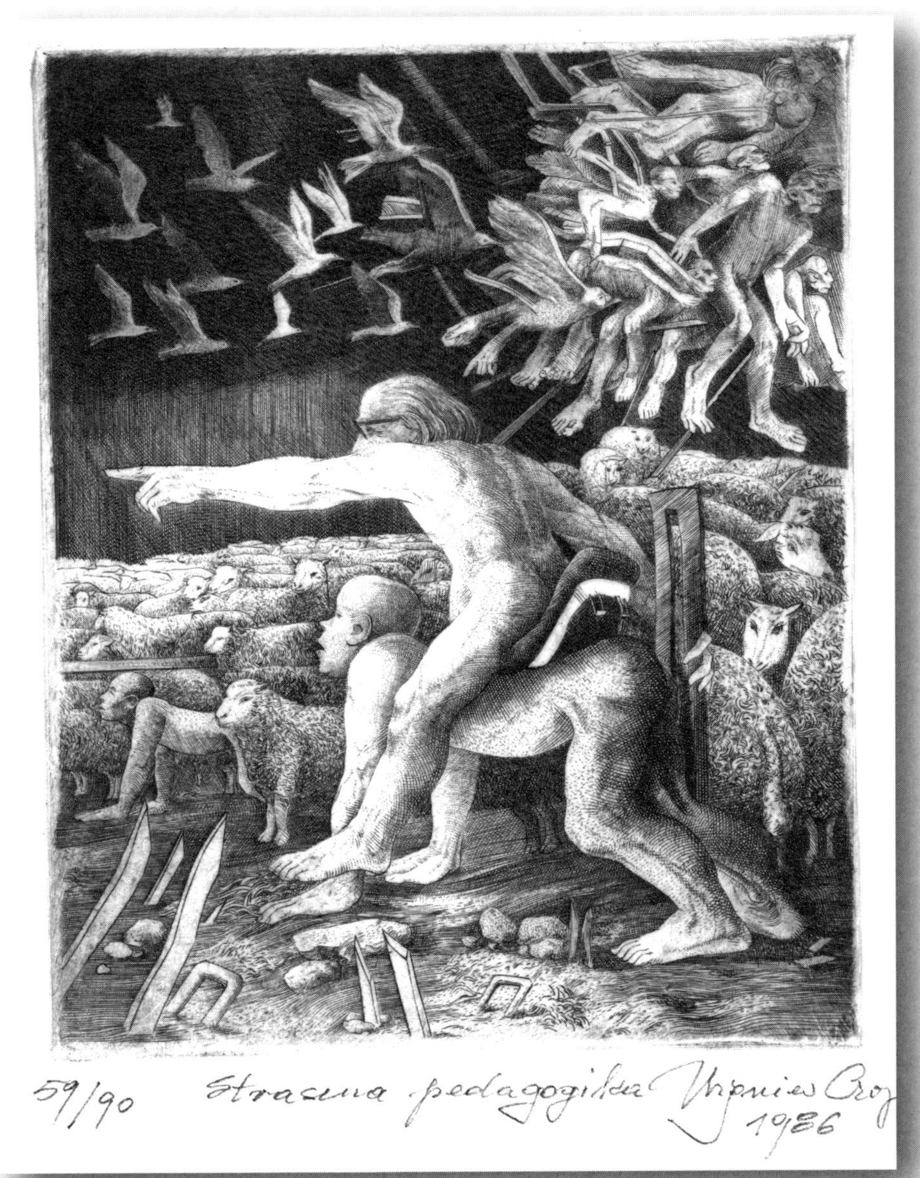

Fig. 61

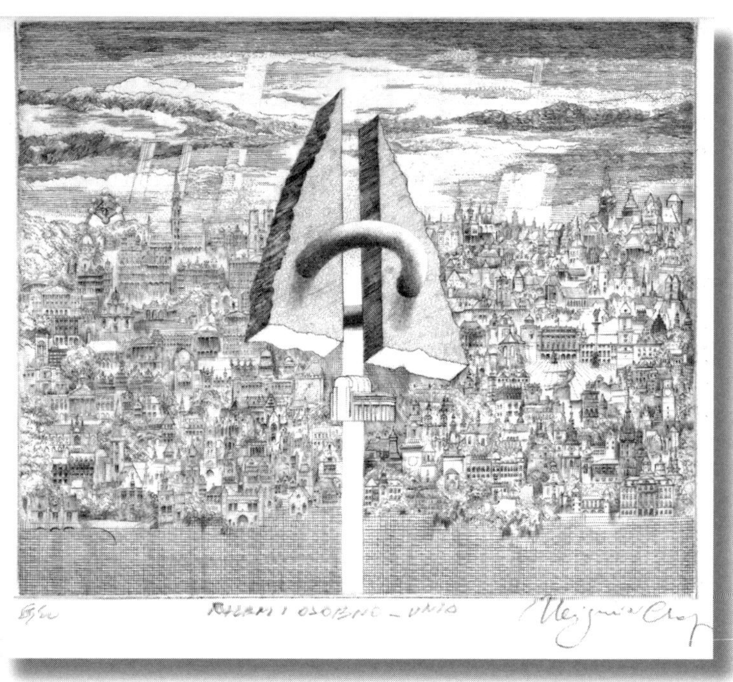

Fig. 54

Daily Invalid Corruption is a series of installations created by me from 1995 onwards. The changes that resulted from the fall of Communism in Europe, including the breakdown of communication barriers, the transformation of society, the all-pervading influence of mass media both in the community and in the daily life of the ordinary citizen, these were the new realities confronting the former East bloc countries. All of these had a major influence on the language and expression of artistic creativity.

Daily Invalid Corruption of 1995 [*Figs.* 40 and 41], deals with the consumerism, which was, almost overnight, thrust into Romania's consciousness. The early 1990s – the dawn of a new world: illusory, confused, aggressive, seductive and dependent.

It should be noted that in the last period of Communism in Romania living conditions were harsh – there was no heat in houses, there was no food in shops (bread and other provisions), and the use of electricity was strictly controlled (children were reading by candlelight). As for information, literature was banned and everything was censored by the Communist party. On public television, two hours per day were taken up with programmes reporting the achievements of Socialism. After a 'Golden Era' had been brought to darkness and humility, December 1989 was like an historical 'Big Bang' with a 'Live Revolution' appearing on televisions around the world – a great big lie that persists even today. The process of revolution is passed on to the next generation, maybe for eternity. Recent Romanian history often documents the blame of this past.

Romania in the 1990s debuts on a NEW field, from regionalization to globalization – a society with no experience fallen in the mall's democracy.

Daily Invalid Corruption illustrates the daily temptations of the 1990s. It provokes discussion on the need for and value of some of the principal objects in the 'New Life' of the society: the refrigerator to fill with food, the TV set which bombards viewers with urgent and useless information, information often false and lying in the case of political information on the period between 1990 and 2000, but also at the same time symbolizing the treatment or cure of the excessive consumption of the new and the fake/false.

As a witness of the society's changes, the author is part of the artistic generation of the 1990s and continues the series of installations, speaking of TRANZIT as transit, transitive, transitory, transition, transitional in terms of the social, political and cultural conditions.

The installation Daily Invalid Corruption of 1995/2008 [*Fig.* 40] continues the investigation and proposes a common model for the contemporary space of daily corruption. To highlight that this is a topic not only in Romania or even in Central and Eastern European countries, the fridge and TV has been recycled from English bulky waste, the fridge containing boxes of paracetamol, the arguably most commonly known pill in Europe.

2007

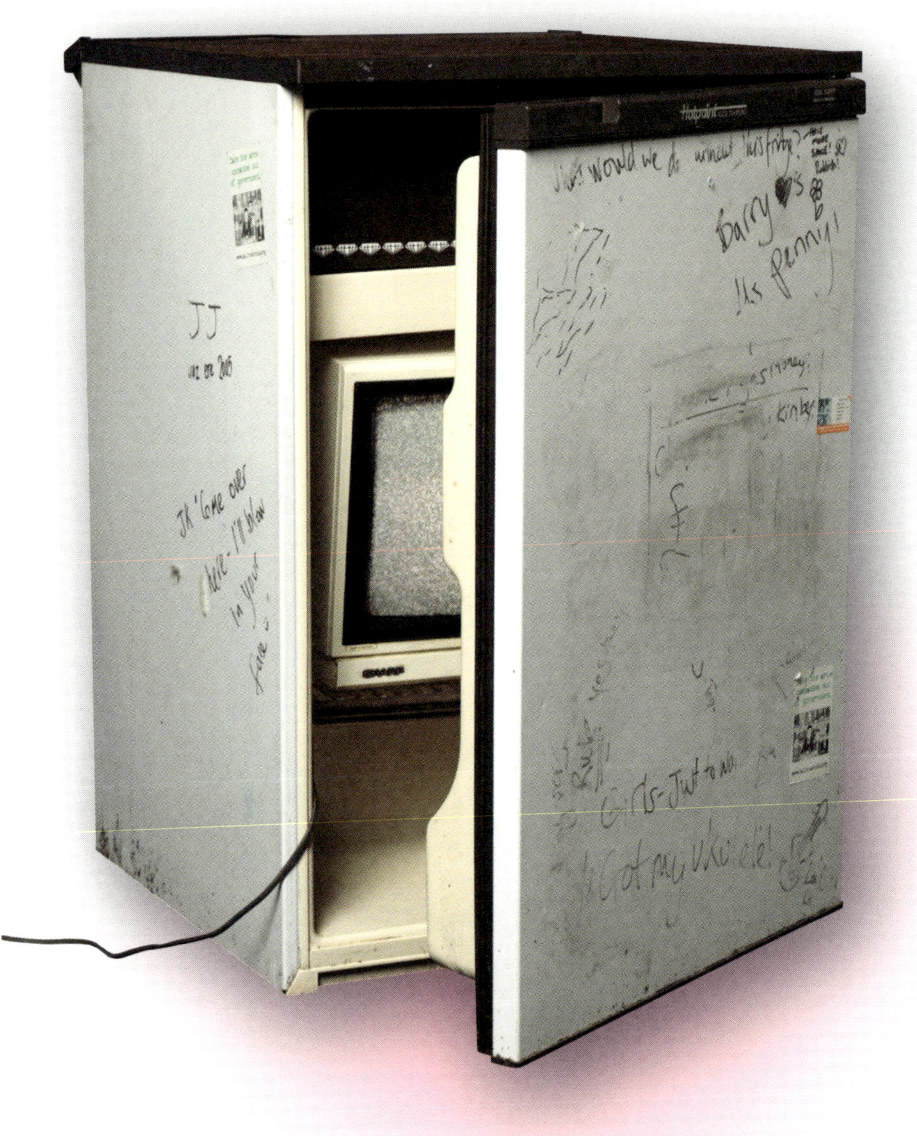

*Fig.*40

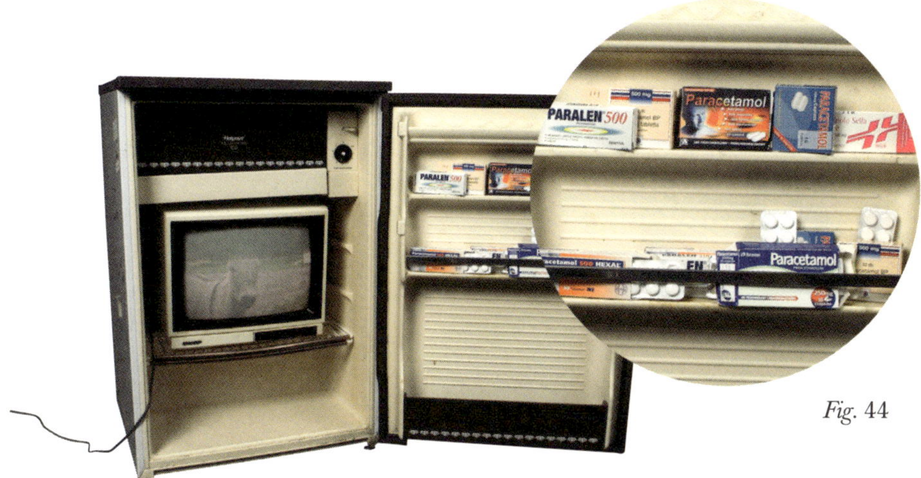

Fig. 44

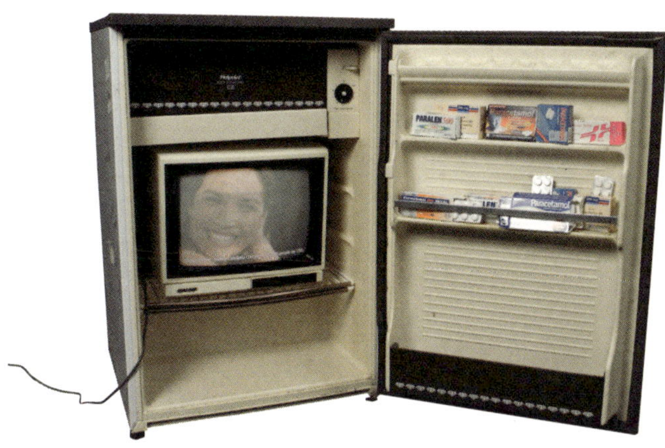

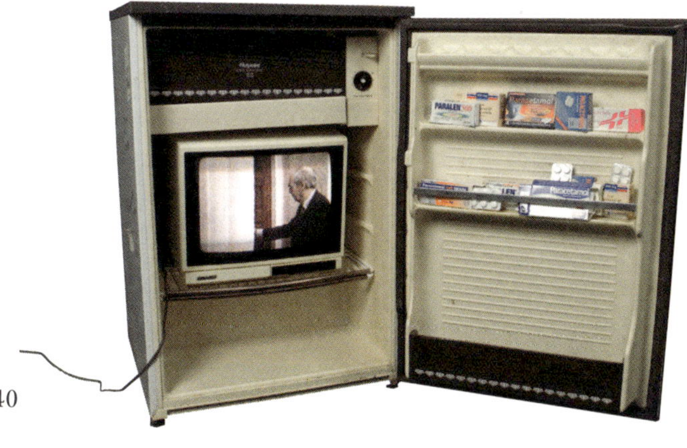

*Fig.*40

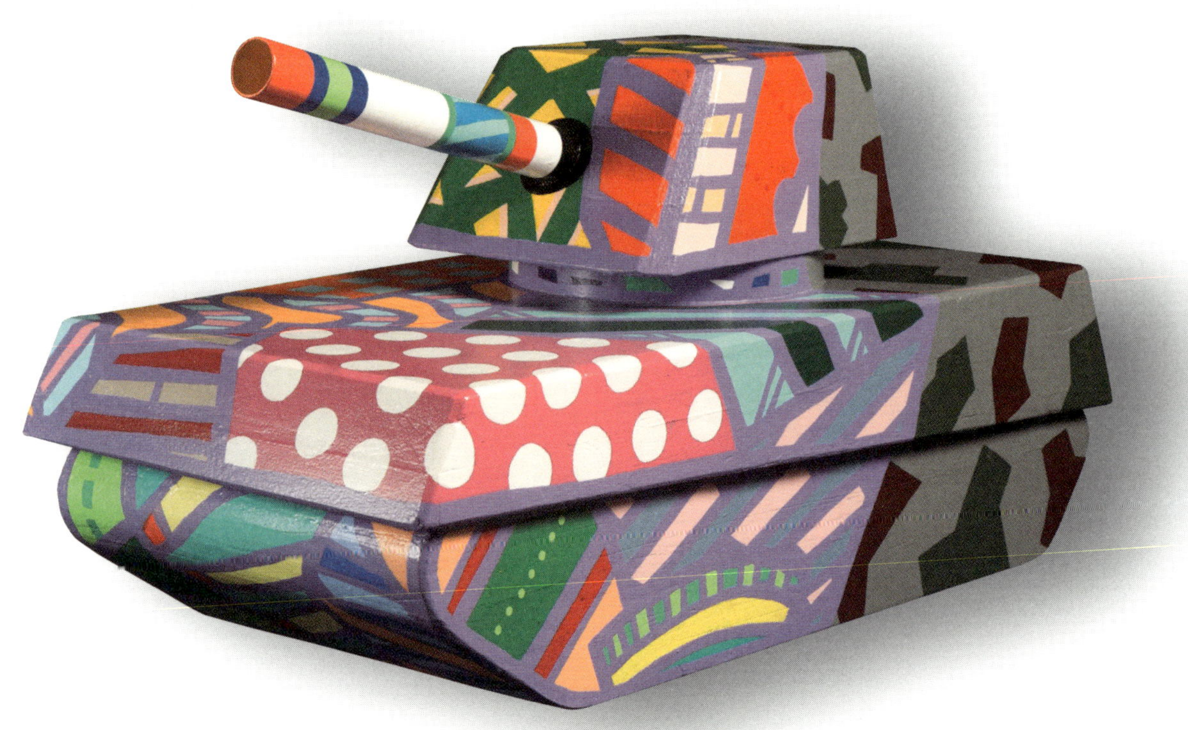

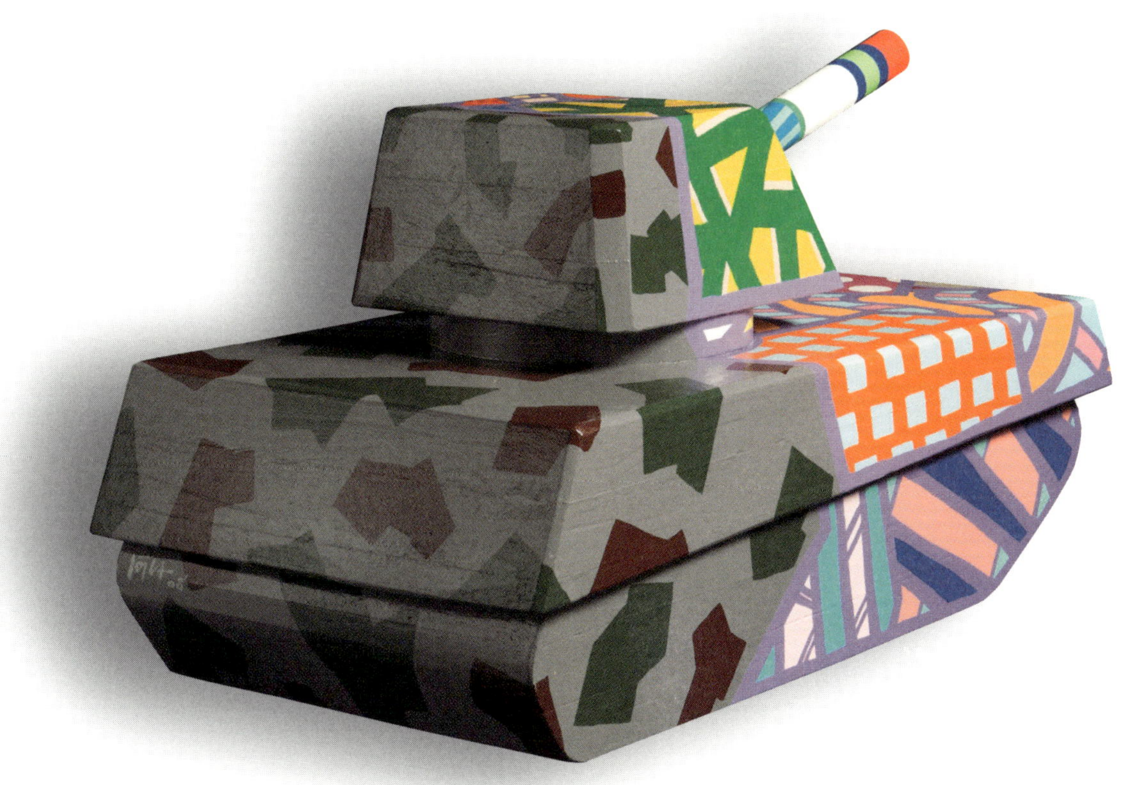

About Dictatorships

Dictatorship is the suppression and liquidation of individuality (of the many in favour of the few), manifesting itself in uniform behaviour.

The act of wearing a uniform – we may take school, professional and military uniforms as examples here – is the culmination of a uniform way of thinking becoming visible. Uniforms are the expression of enforced conformity of design and colour. It is the individual who wears the uniform, though. The purpose of the uniform is to make visible the potential individual behaviour of its bearer while hiding the latter's individuality behind the adapted form.

Individuality Versus Dictatorship of 2008 [*Fig.* 28] consists of a tank, a symbol of suppression and extermination and usually camouflaged creating stealth. Camouflage is characteristic of destruction – like the tank, it hides its intentions. Only the impact of accomplished actions looms large and can be made visible.

As a result individuality has to be conceptualized as its direct opposite. Individuality wants to be visible and strives after recognition. Bright colours and different patterns deprive the tank of its invisibility, thereby making it defenceless and worthless. 'Dictatorship' is overcome. Individuality, personality and diversity take the place of 'uniformity'.

To sum up: the more society, or the human being, is marked by individuality, the less prone it is to fall victim to unified structures which automatically bring suppression. Mental and emotional monoculture leads to comparable results, similar to those found in agriculture.

It should not be forgotten that dictatorial structures do not only appear in social processes but may also have effects in all areas where individuals meet and interact, even within marriages and families.

2007

A group of 15 pictures, primarily depicting the city's landmark the Brandenburg Gate throughout three decades, forms the hub of *Time Travels* of 2008 [*Fig.*10]. Expressive images both old (on the left) and new (on the right) flank it. They not only cover public behaviour of the former ruling state bureaucracy, but also show some extremes of today's freedom: in an 'anything-goes' type of society, the possibilities of today are yesterday's unthinkables.

Cuckoos meet at Alexanderplatz to find a stage to present themselves, human beings as artworks. The concept of my contribution aims to contrast the ruling ideology of dictatorship with the prevailing consumerism of democracy. What were emotions then are sentiments today.

The main focus of the block is a photograph of the Brandenburg Gate taken in the 1980s: people staring over the cordons into the West, their hearts full of yearning. This was the magic point of the compass where our city, our country, our world came to an end; where it just began for others, though. A second snapshot taken on 22 December 1989 depicts people running through the gate. On this very day it was officially opened for pedestrian border crossings. People ran out into the world. The earth turned into the globe again.

My contribution is composed in a way to illustrate the changes both in the cityscape and in people's minds. Much redevelopment has taken place, but it has resulted in a good deal of sterilization that has altered the life of the city's inhabitants. In the Prenzlauer Berg district, new but ugly glass and steel buildings are increasingly creeping into empty spaces left behind from the last World War; what comes into being there is state-of-the-art architecture that is unaffordable for most people as rents are soaring.

In a way the grey dreariness of the past had its own charm after all; but most of it has been lost for good. Just a few of the redevelopment areas have created a new quality that is worth speaking of. For me personally, to think and act freely is the greatest achievement that came with the changes in government.

2007

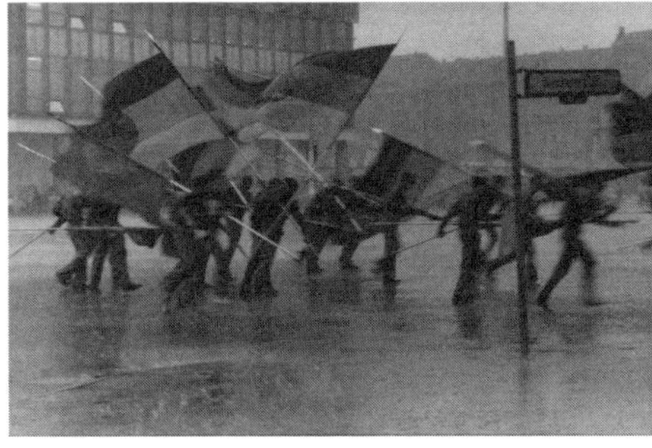

Berlin, 1 May 1987
Fig. 22

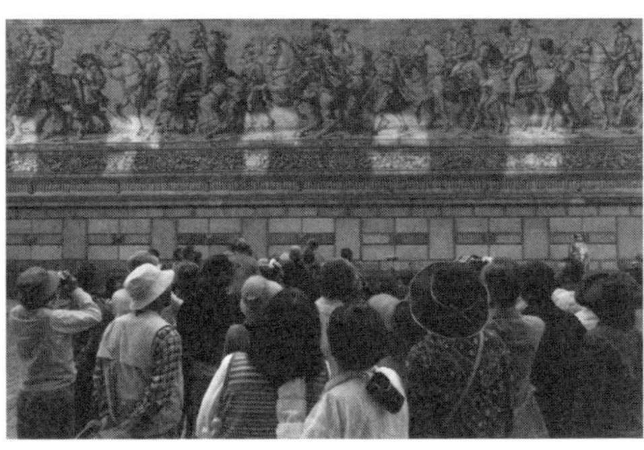

Procession of the Dukes, Dresden 2005
Fig. 25

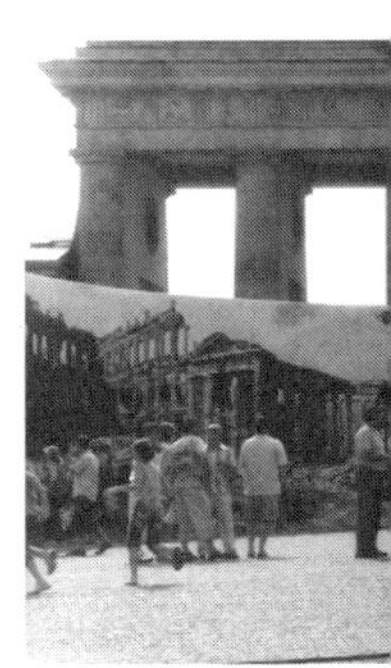

Pariser

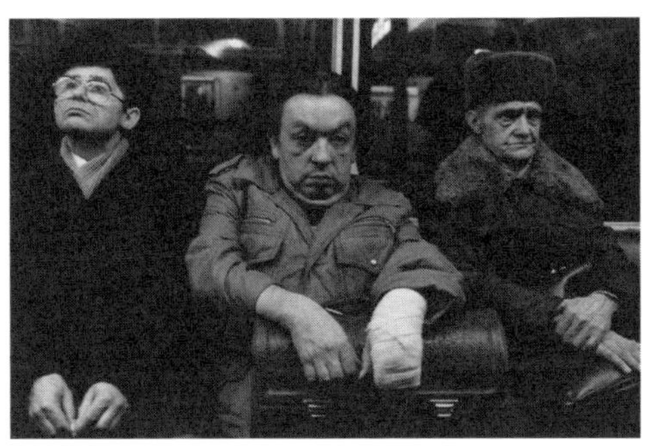

Underground Line A, Berlin 1986
Fig. 24

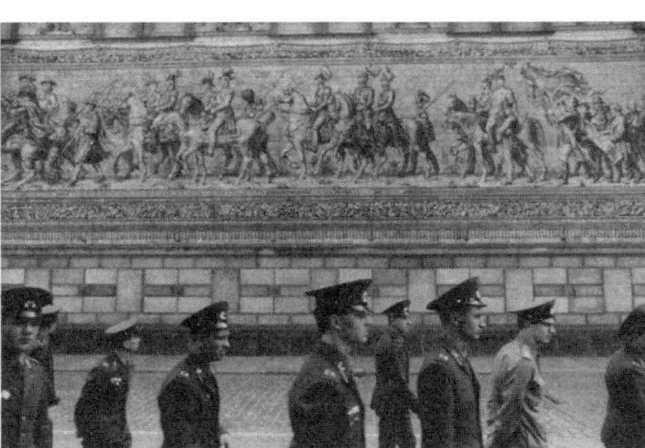

Procession of the Dukes, Dresden 1984
Fig. 18

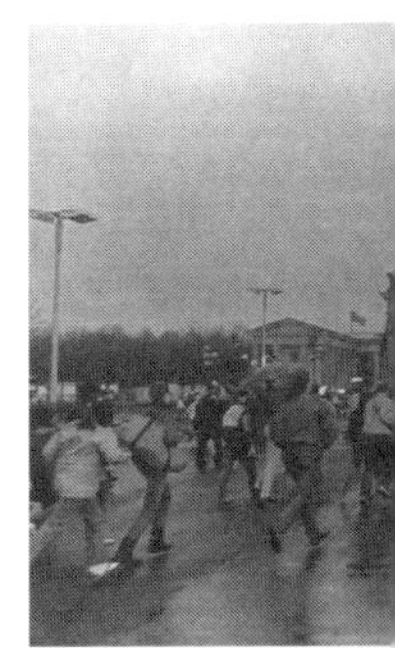

Brandenburg

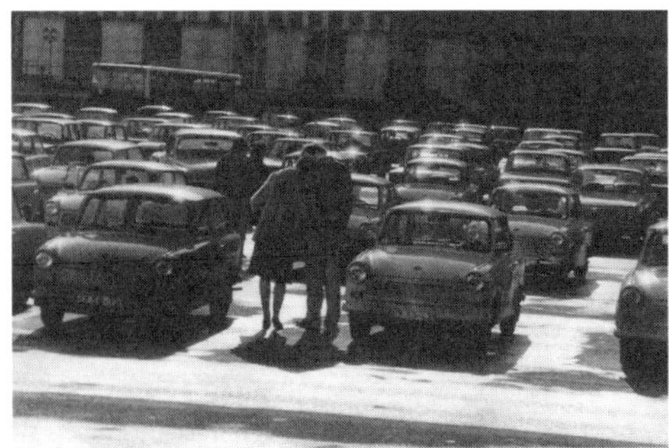

Schlossplatz, Berlin 1982
Fig. 17

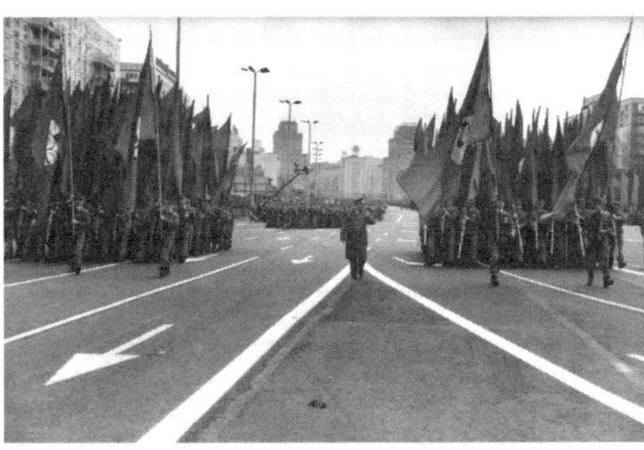

Berlin 1 May, 1989
Fig. 23

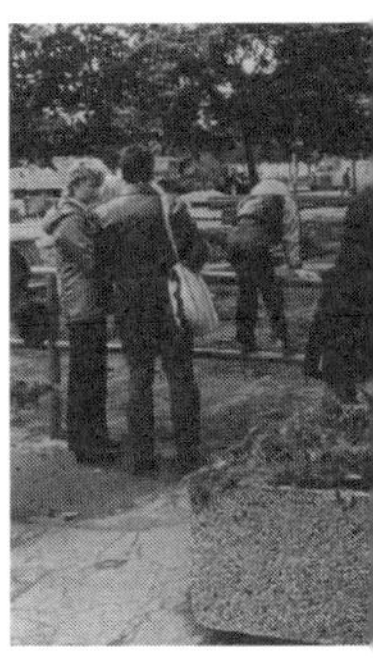

Brandenb

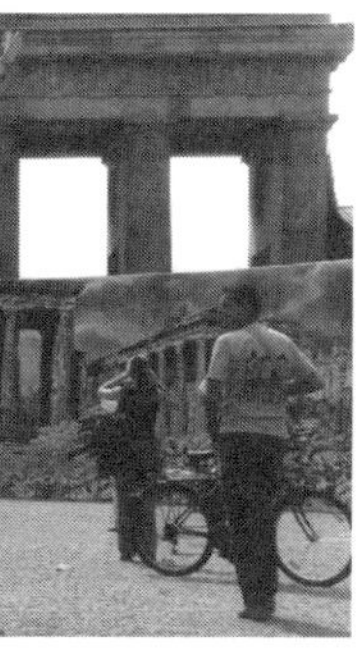

n 2005

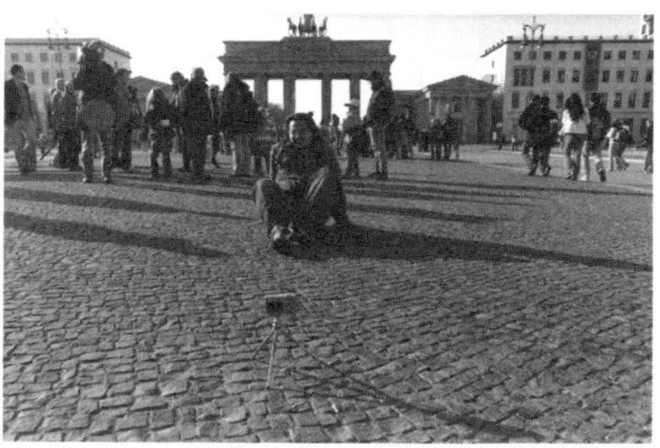

Brandenburg Gate, Berlin 2005
Fig. 16

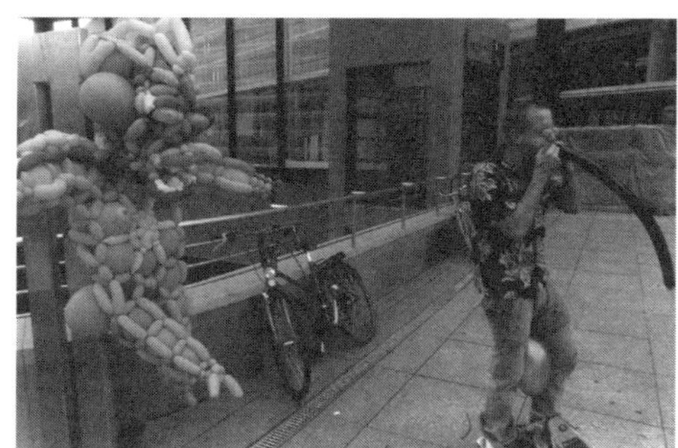

Potsdamer Platz, Berlin 2005
Fig. 19

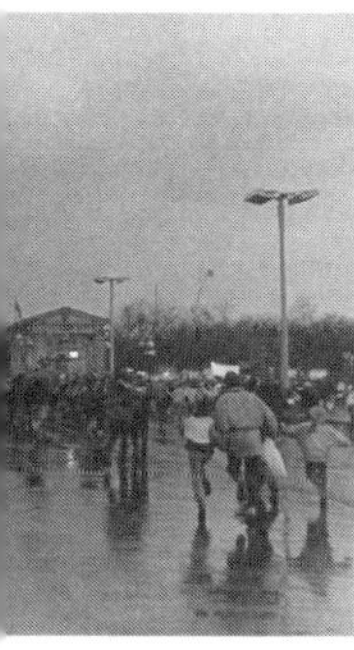

22 Dec. 1989

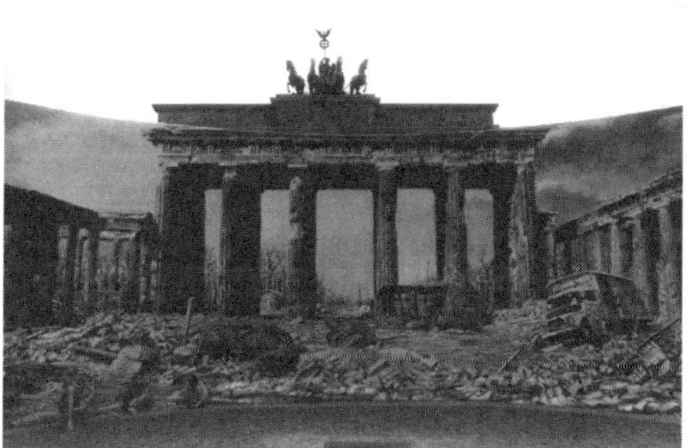

Brandenburg Gate, Berlin 2005
Fig. 14

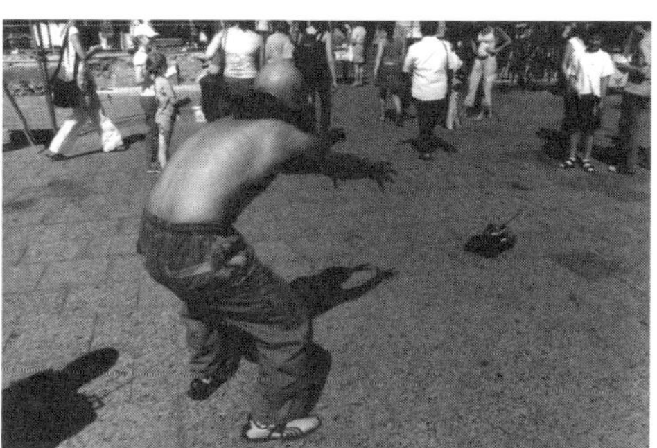

Alexanderplatz, Berlin 2006
Fig. 20

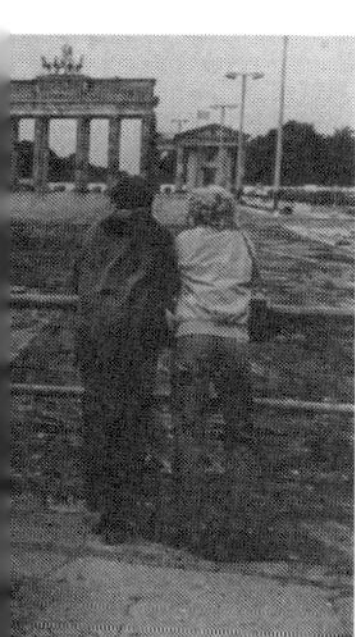

lin 1982

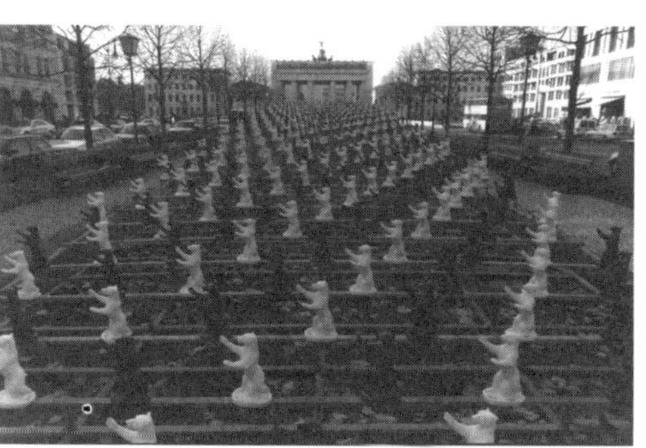

Brandenburg Gate, Berlin 2000
Fig. 15

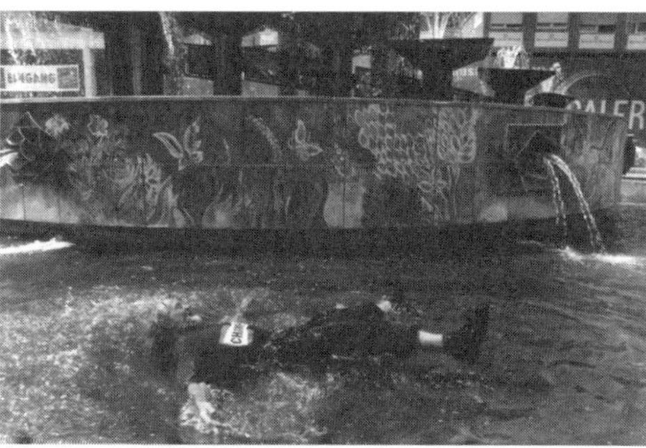

Alexanderplatz, Berlin 2006
Fig. 21

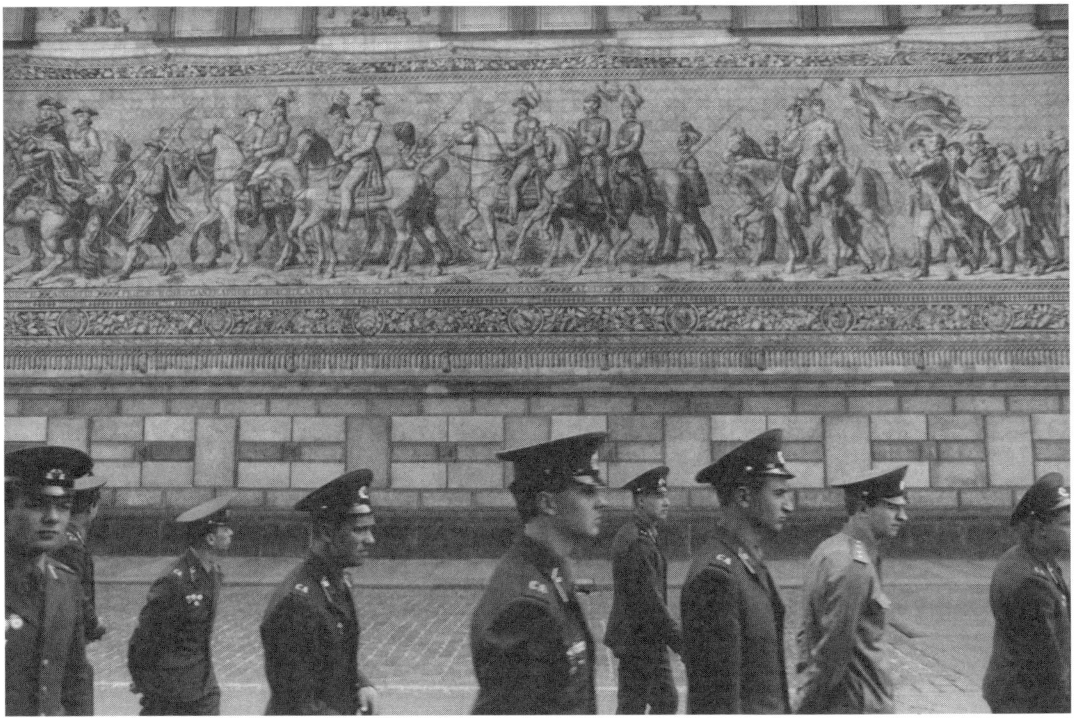

     Harald Hauswald, <u>Procession of the Dukes, Dresden 1984</u>
<u>Procession of the Dukes, Dresden 2005</u>

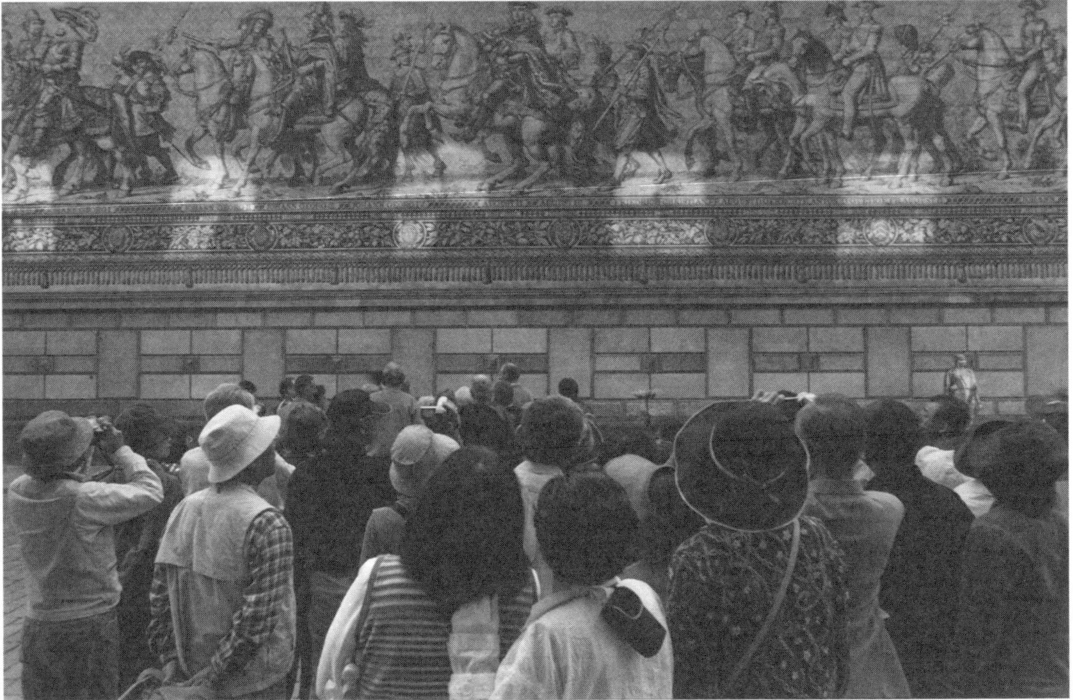

Fig. 18

Fig. 25

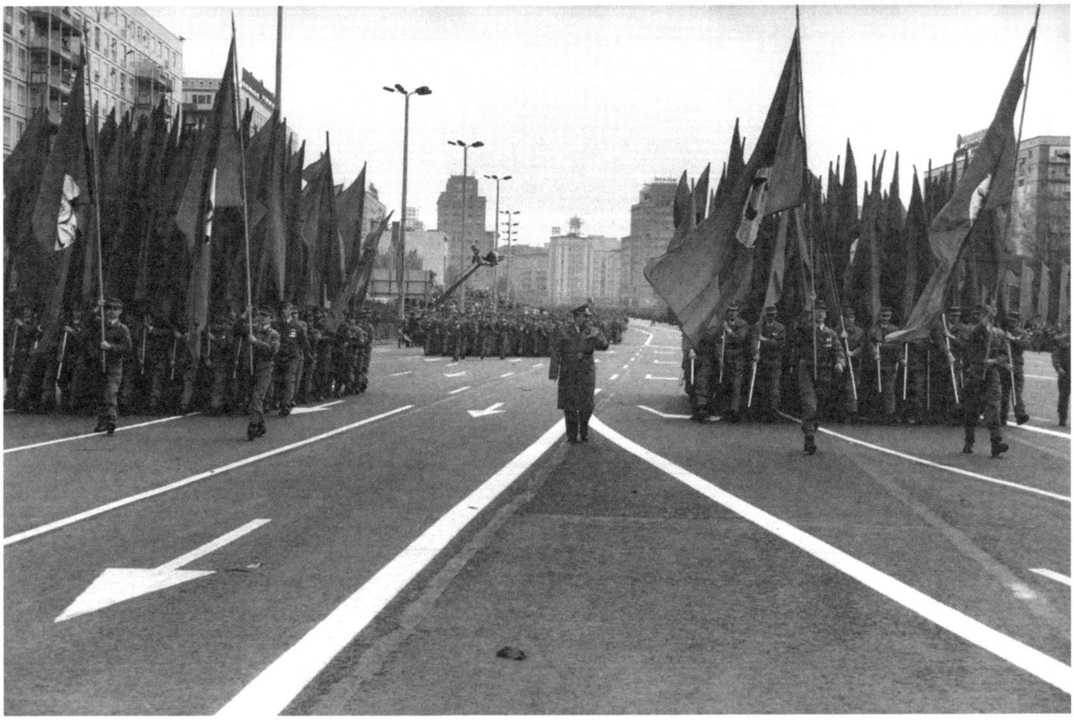

   Berlin 1 May, 1989
Schlossplatz, Berlin 1982

all photographs part of Time Travels

Fig. 23

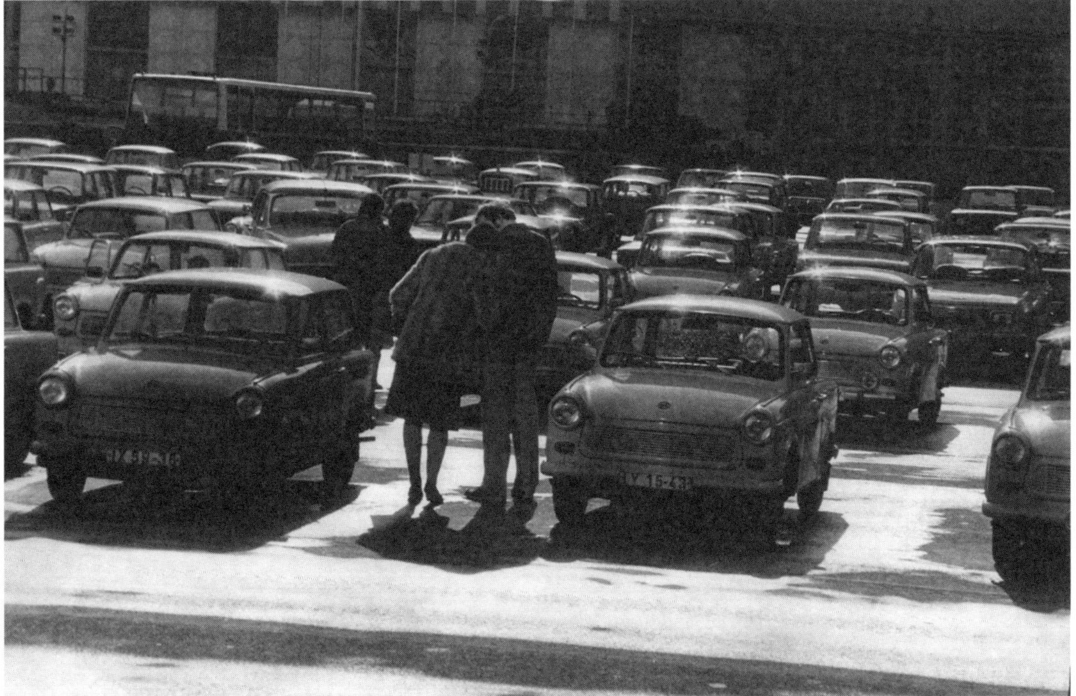

Fig. 17

  Harald Hauswald, <u>Brandenburg Gate, Berlin 22 Dec. 1989</u> (part of <u>Time Travels</u>)

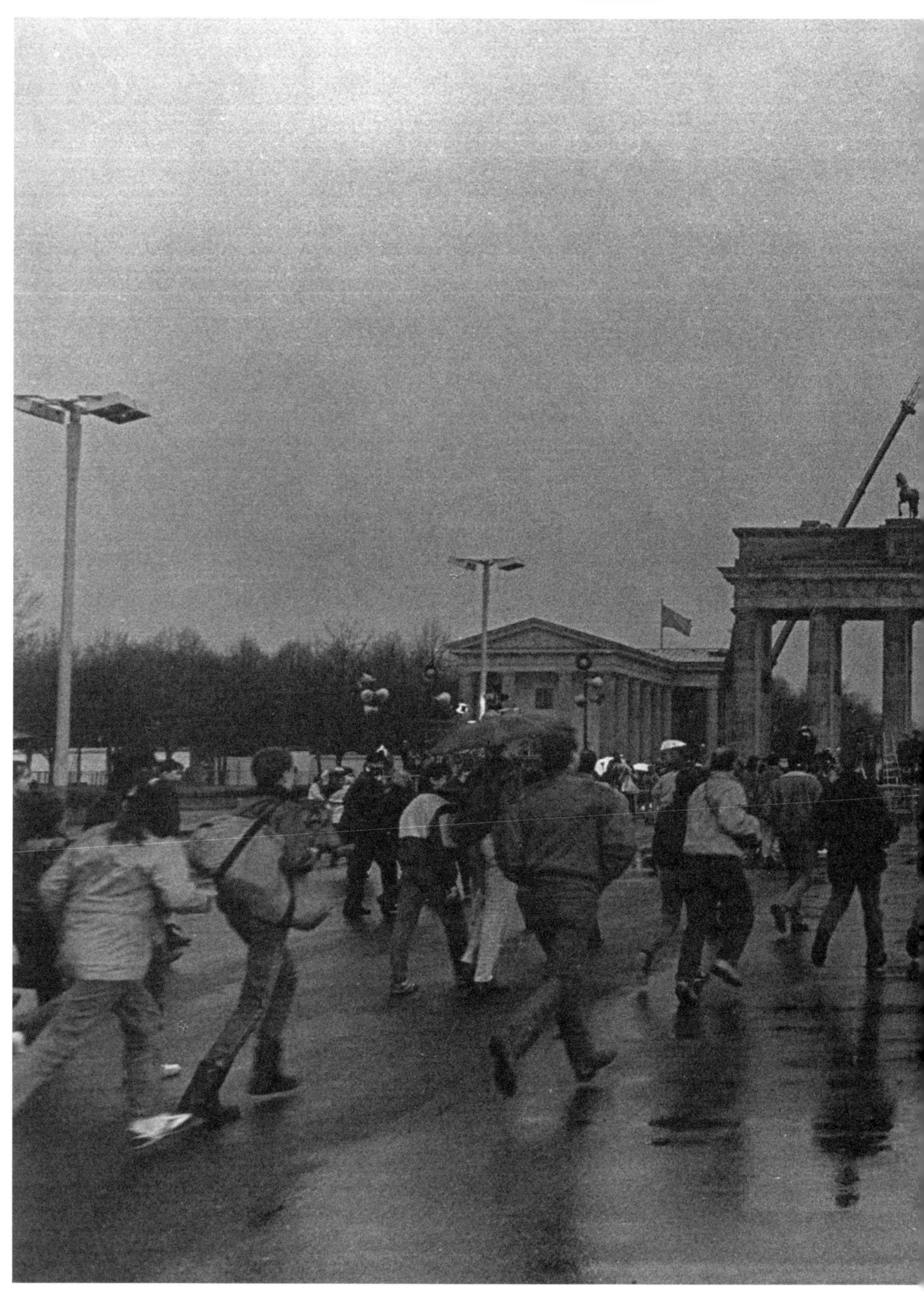

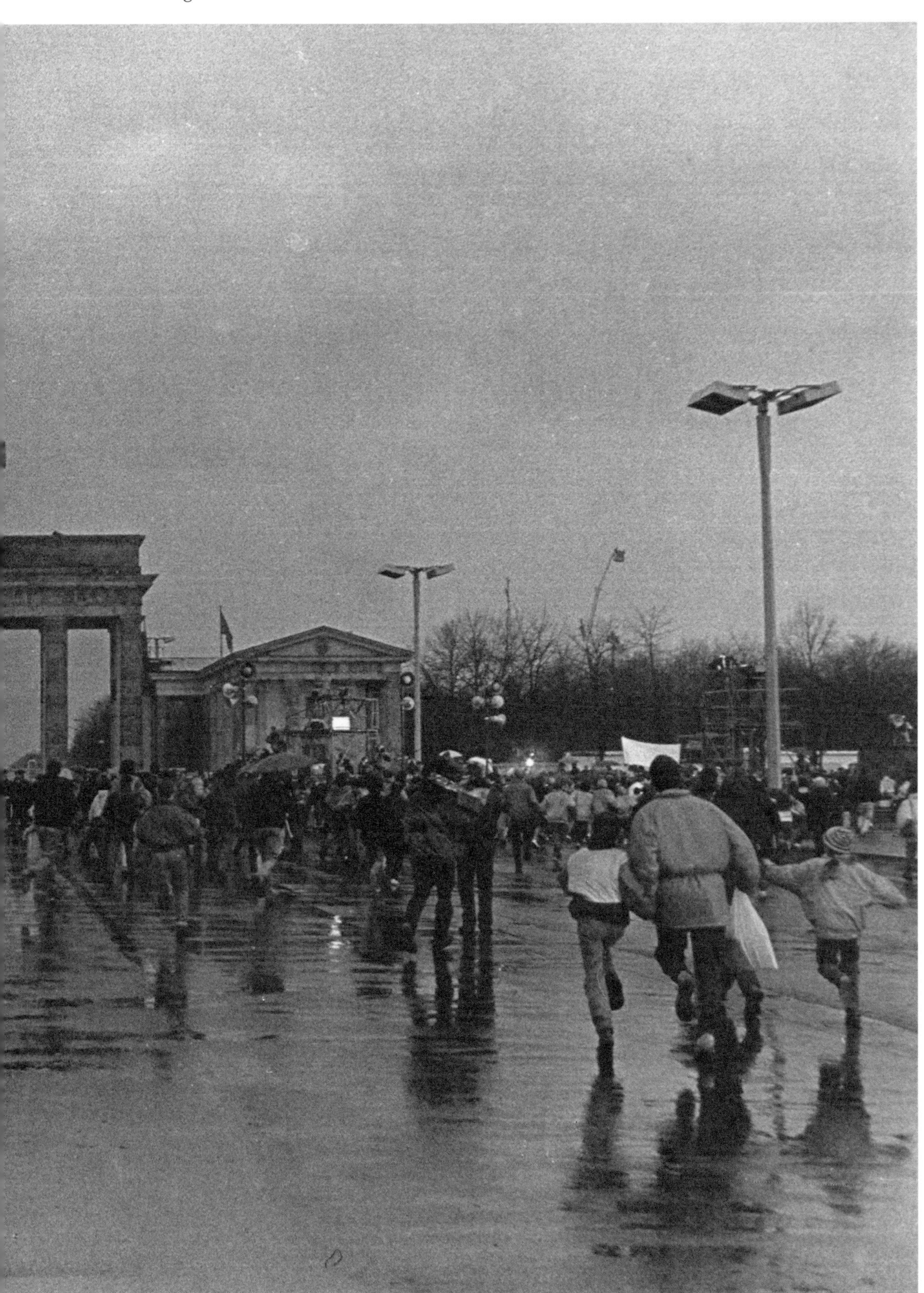

   Harald Hauswald, Underground Line A, Berlin 1986 (part of Time Travels)

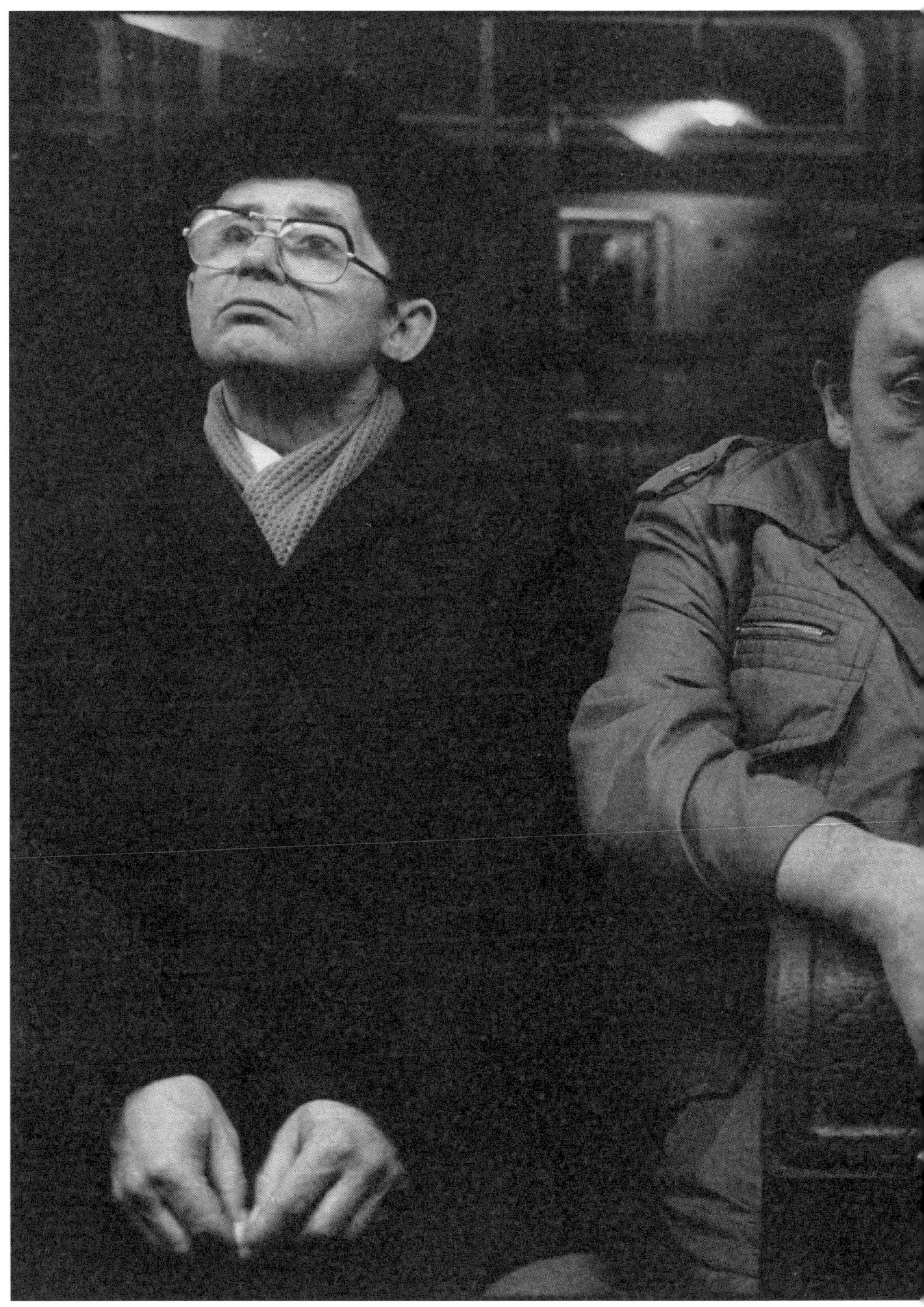

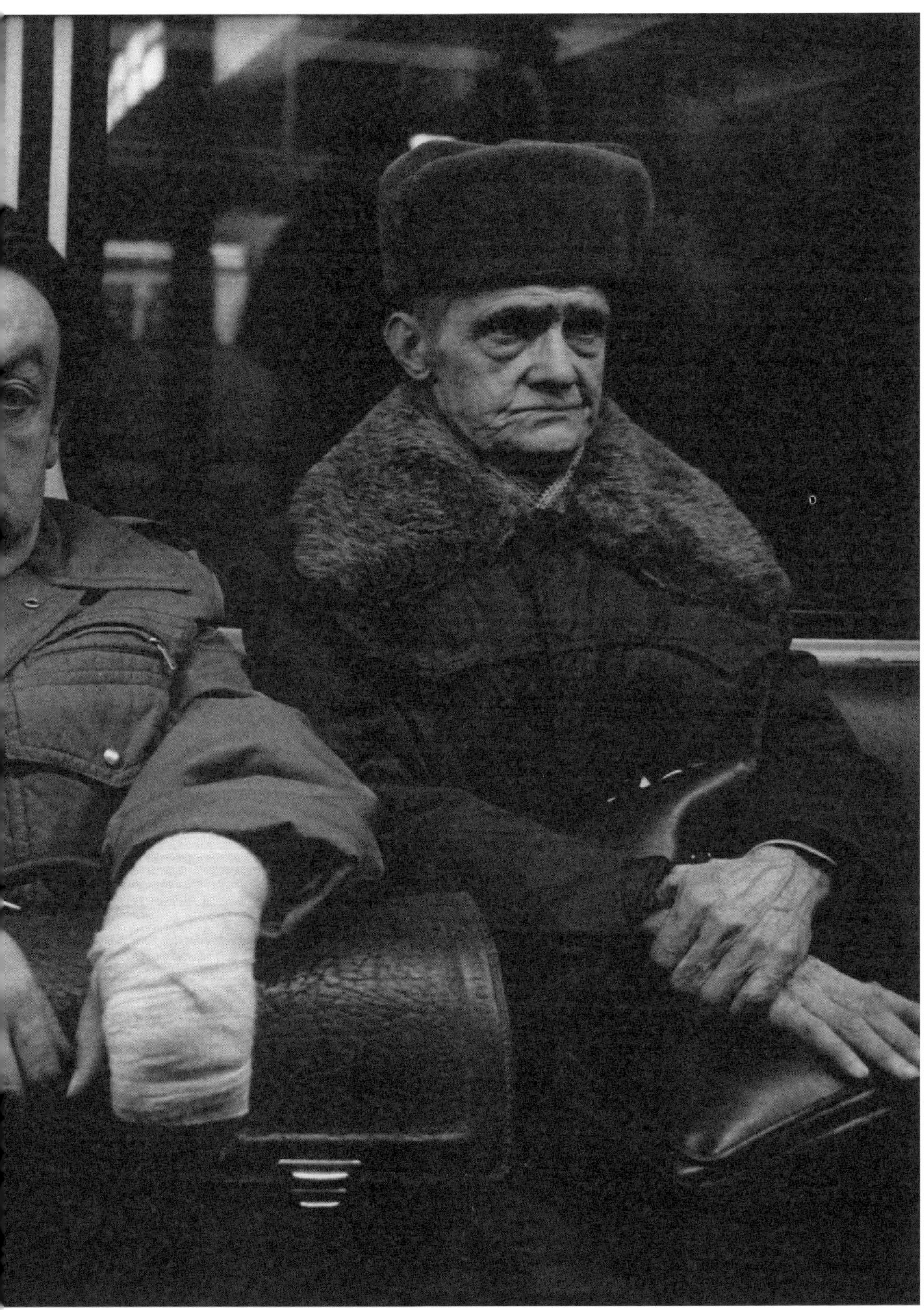

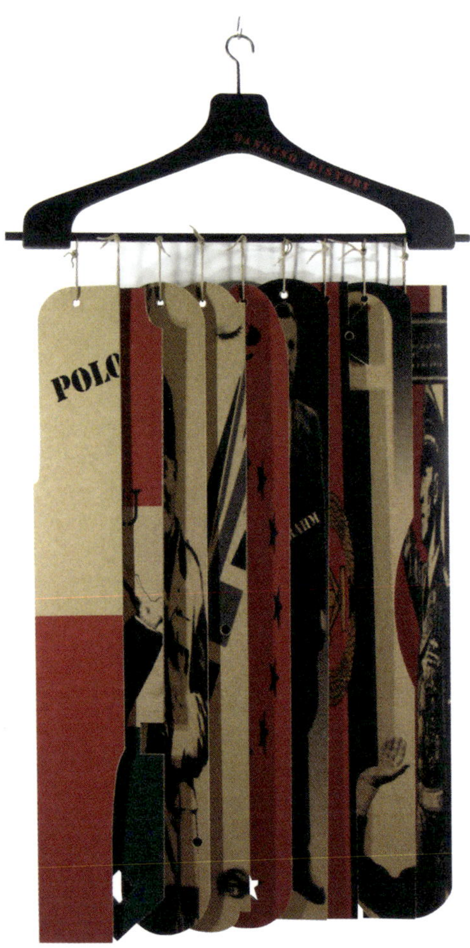
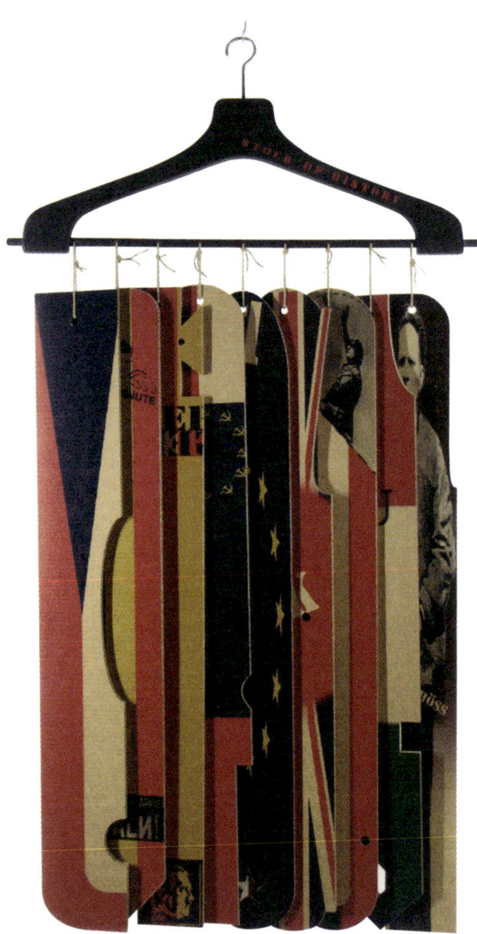

Fig. 33

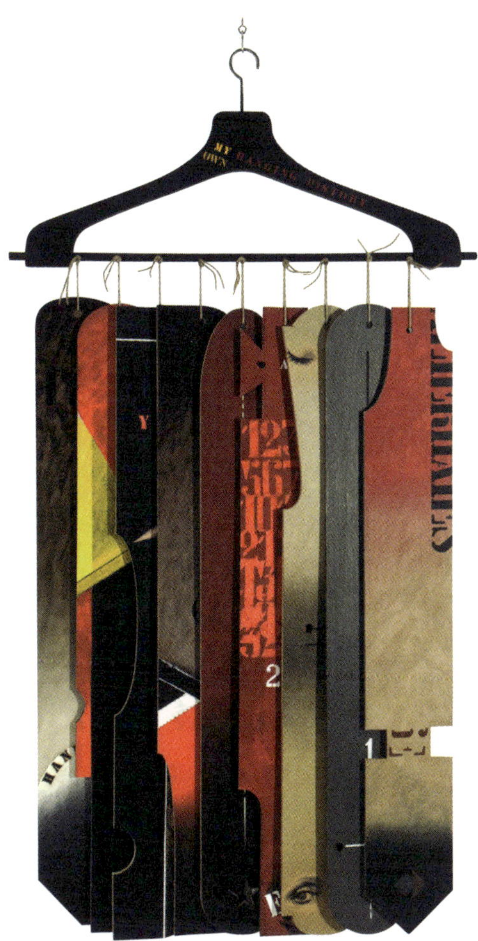
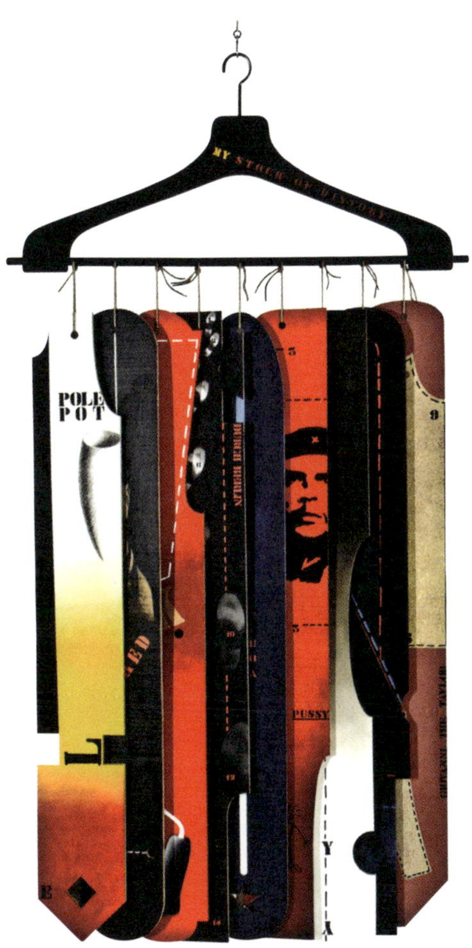

Fig. 35

My Work – My Life

My creative effort aims to classify all those things that make up the visual store and the existential memory of the world. I am fascinated by the work of people, their 'fingerprints' left unconsciously during their work; I am magnetized just as much by the blacksmith's and carpenter's workbench as I am by the bureaucrat's desk; I am fascinated by their procedures, and by the 'metrics' they have dedicated to their own functions. Their numbers, their letters and their gestures mark my compositions with a taxonomical frame; they are paratactical seals that make the syntax of the work vibrate – visual or chromatic flashes, but also intriguing questions and secret formulae of a cabalistic mathematics. They are traces of actions that have been, and that in my work regenerate in the negative of the idea-model template. I do not set any limits on the use of the techniques that I regard as necessary to give shape to my ideas.

Everything belongs to me, from drawing to watercolour, from oil painting to photography, even to installations. The techniques are always mixed: assembly of objects, often cut out of wood or cardboard with laser techniques from electronic files or freehand, copper supports oxidized by acids, or canvas and cardboard and, finally, acrylic or oil painting. Often digital photography plays a part, suitably camouflaged, 'with an old look' I would say, in the form of both collage and direct printing on various supports. Three-dimensional elements play in the watercolours, strings that hang like visual filters between the eye and the picture on paper, expressly prepared by a paper manufacturer. The three-dimensionality, which in the installation or in the collage arises from the volumes of the objects, is obtained here by the tonal play of the lights and the shadows, with the pictorial scanning of the planes and of the levels. And, finally, the clothes hangers from which hang silhouettes of improbable tailoring, fascinating objectual etymologies of the world that surrounds us, the result of a process of both ideation and observation which has led me to rearrange concepts and memories of past things and times, to rebuild here the phantasmatic bodies of the objects exposed: archives of the memory, faces and symbols of human horror, accumulative sequences of geography and history, simulacra of political entropies. All are entrusted to dissimulative silhouettes in cardboard, hanging in the air, balanced on mobile hooks, grouped together like clothes in a wide-open wardrobe or on exhibition in a particular kind of *wunderkammer*, which again can gather together, and look after, the multiple signs of past and present horrors.

The work is framed in a systematic encyclopaedic project, with which for eight years I have dedicated my time to making an inventory of this, and depicting the shape of the things in the category of an enormous 'still life', or, better, of 'a reality in pose', reproduced also by connotative fragments, according to the specular logic of fractals. This reality is from time to time de-structured and re-structured on the basis of a clear formal rigour, made up of natural elements and functional objects, of affection and seduction. The omnivorous power of the ostentatious objects, which are the last threshold of reification of the subject, like alarming signs of gradual estrangement is increasingly typical of the prevailing standardization of our systems of life. Yet it is also a criticism of the drifting of our daily existence – whether it be a real or virtual subspecies – accepted as a sterile ideology which prevents us from facing an 'unforgettable' history of Europe.

2007

Vlad Nancă

I Do Not Know What Union I Want to Belong to Anymore is a work I
created in 2003 after noticing that the Romanian flag was always proudly
positioned alongside the European Union flag in Romanian official
institutions [*Fig.*55]. Government buildings, army bases, but also
churches, kindergartens and schools were all displaying the EU flag
(some even the NATO flag). It struck me how up until 1989 the Romanian
flag had always been placed next to the red flag with the hammer and
sickle. Back in 2003 Romania wasn't even a member of the EU.
However, the need to associate itself with a greater power was obvious.
Somehow stuck between mentalities and the rights and the wrongs of
the two unions, I really didn't know where I wanted to belong, hence I
shifted the colours of the flags to underline the confusion and this need
to be allied with a greater power. In 2004, when Pat Cox, then president
of the European Parliament visited Bratislava, he saw my work exhibited
in a bill-board art project and commented how the two unions could
never be compared. I would say that immoral power schemes and
corrupt economic and political systems are equally strong and wrong,
no matter the Union, and they could be equally as oppressive and unfair
to the population.

Four years after that work and 18 years after the end of Communism
in Eastern Europe I had the chance to be part of a series of encounters
in different European countries under the title 'Overcoming Dictatorships.' The various lectures, presentations and debates, but mostly
remembering and rememorizing recent history through testimonies, have
brought new ideas and more clarity on my beliefs.

Ideal of 2007 [*Fig.*57]. In 1956 during the Hungarian revolution the
communist symbols were torn out of the flags leaving a whole in the
middle. The same liberating gesture was repeated in 1989, first in Germany and then in Romania. For a few days, in each of these countries
the national flag was not only without an emblem but also with a hole in
the middle. To me this is a symbol of pure freedom, something that
could only happen in times of strong spiritual engagement and idealistic
fervour. By putting the three flags together I am aiming to realize a spiritual union that surpasses time, history and borders. The three countries
(and their flags) are connected by the emptiness of the middle of the
flag, a spiritual union of genuine revolutionary freedom, where no symbols
spoil the essence of those days of liberty. It is an *Ideal* union I wish I
could belong to.

2008

Erden Kosova (submitted by the artist in 2008)

I Do Not Know What Union I Want to Belong to Anymore illustrates the
confusion of the continuities and ruptures in Romania's near past and
future [*Fig.*55]. The dizzying shift between the two, once warring ideological continents, the state-Communism of Eastern Europe and liberal
social democracy of Western Europe is being represented in that piece
by two flags. One of them bears the sickle and hammer combination
used by the USSR and the other has the circular twelve stars of the EU.
Will the latter truly replace the former? Is EU membership really the
only viable alternative for Romania-in-transition, still trying to heal the
traumas of its nightmarish past? Does the coercive reformatting of the
country somehow reiterate the overregulations of bureaucratic communism? Nancă's sardonic swapping of the colours of the two flags (blue
and yellow USSR flag and red and yellow EU flag) points to the
confusion in Romanians' minds with regard to their national identity
through the graphic split of the national tricolour into the insignia of two
transnational entities.

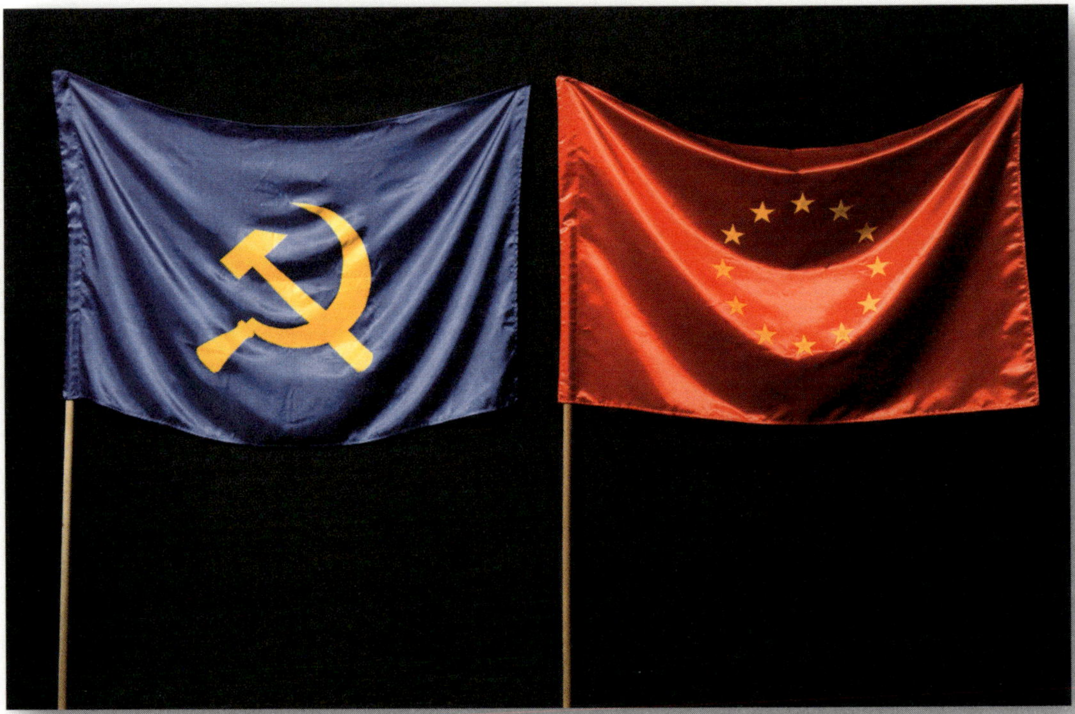

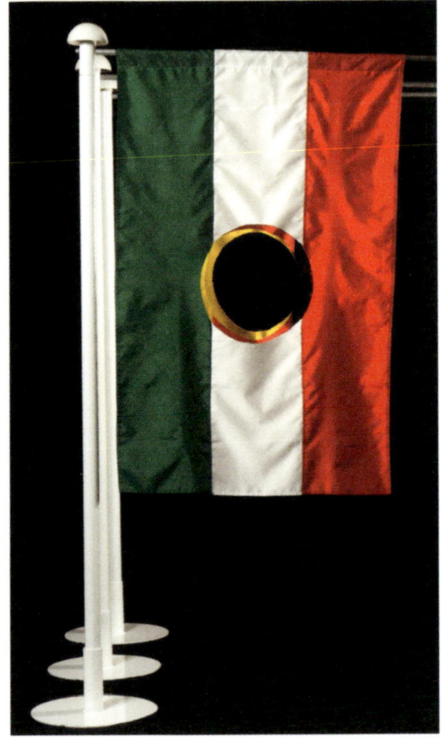

Fig. 55

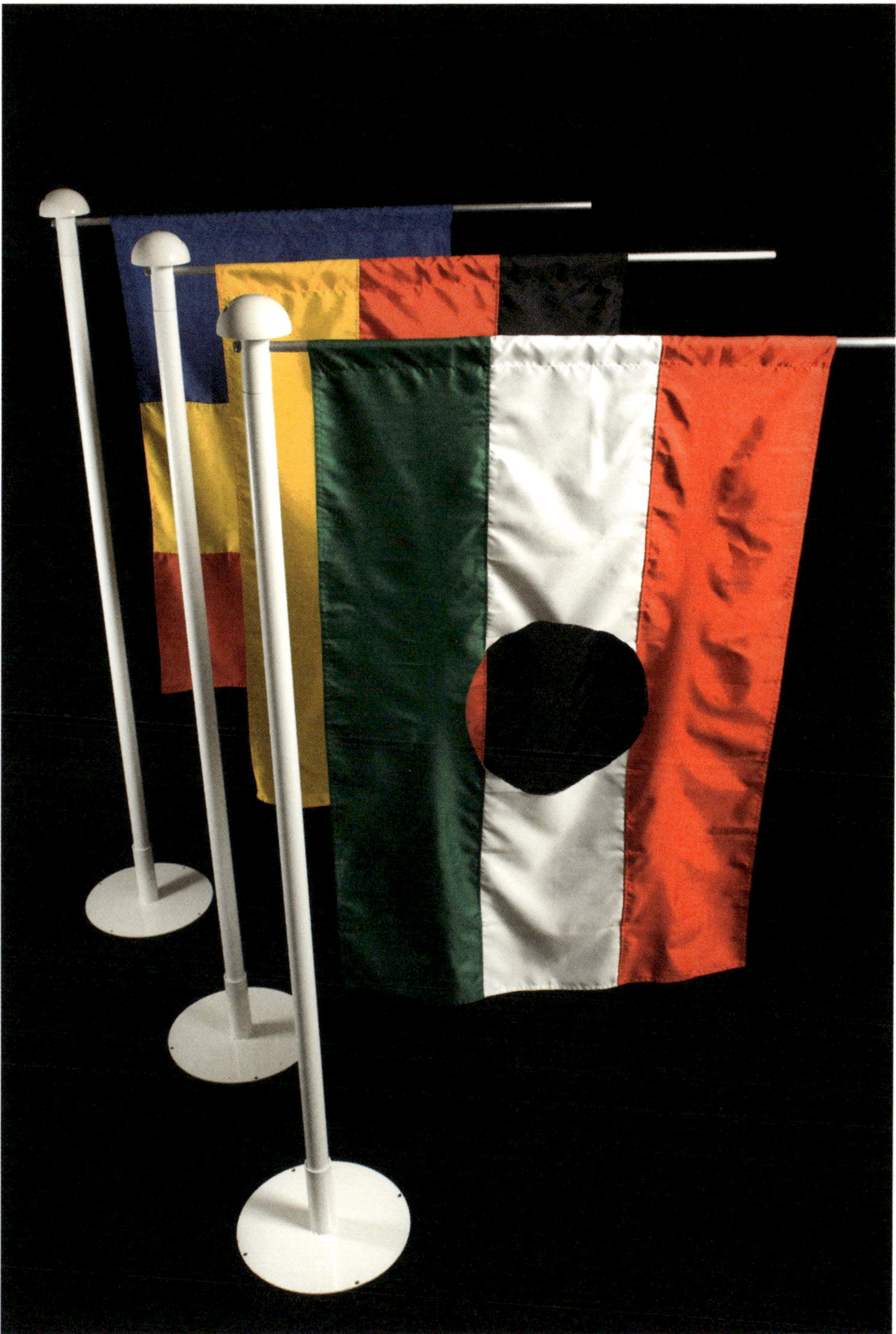

Fig. 57

In 1972 I had a long conversation with one of my artist friends about the possibility of creating artworks in a way that would make it plain that they could only have been produced in Hungary, or in the Eastern Europe of the 1970s. It was almost a given that the five-point star, the sickle and the hammer would be the motifs to be used, as they were the most ubiquitous symbols at the time. My first attempts involved the star and the cobblestone producing works such as *Star (Cobblestone)* of 1973 [*Fig.*27]; then, in 1973, I 'picked up' the sickle and the hammer. I showed them, I raised them in front of my face, and I photographed myself with them in several series; then I transferred these photographs to silkscreen prints, one of which became one of the pair of *Almost 30 Years* [*Fig.*26]. These compositions revealed the isolation from the world and the crucifixion and the shackling of the gesture, in a way that rhymed with numerous art-historical preliminaries. But even more importantly, through this act I tried to remove all the unnecessary political overtones that these symbols had acquired. I felt that I had to offload the ideological burden that these objects had collected and then to reinstate them in their fundamental role. A few years later many people thought that this gesture constituted one of the most powerful icons of that age and of Eastern European existence.

These compositions had several variants, with some versions executed in photography and some painted over. In the 1990s I made the so-called 'double pictures', which essentially juxtaposed my older works with a recent composition. I tried to find out how they reacted to each other. In 1999, I completed a 'sickle and hammer' series, where the two tools flew off, leaving behind empty spaces. These compositions reflect the constant movement of history and life, creating a new kind of interrelationship.

The other part of *Almost 30 Years* was executed in 2002 [*Fig.*26], repeating the pose originally used in the 1970s. The 29 years that had passed between the taking of the two photographs left deep marks on the lives of people in Hungary. Many things changed after the political transition, and people's attention turned to new structures and new directions. The values became different, or perhaps we think differently about values. The gesture and the movement remained the same, but the two tools have fallen out of the tightly clutched hands, which are now frantically grasping the empty space. Perhaps one day the palms will open and the arms crossed in front of the chest will resemble the ancient gesture of greeting. The portrait shows the joys and the aggravations of the past 29 years, along with the physical changes, the hardships and the anxieties of the times, mixed with a touch of ironic sardonicism.

The twin pictures record the conditions both as they were then and as they are now, holding up a faithful mirror to the spectator.

2007

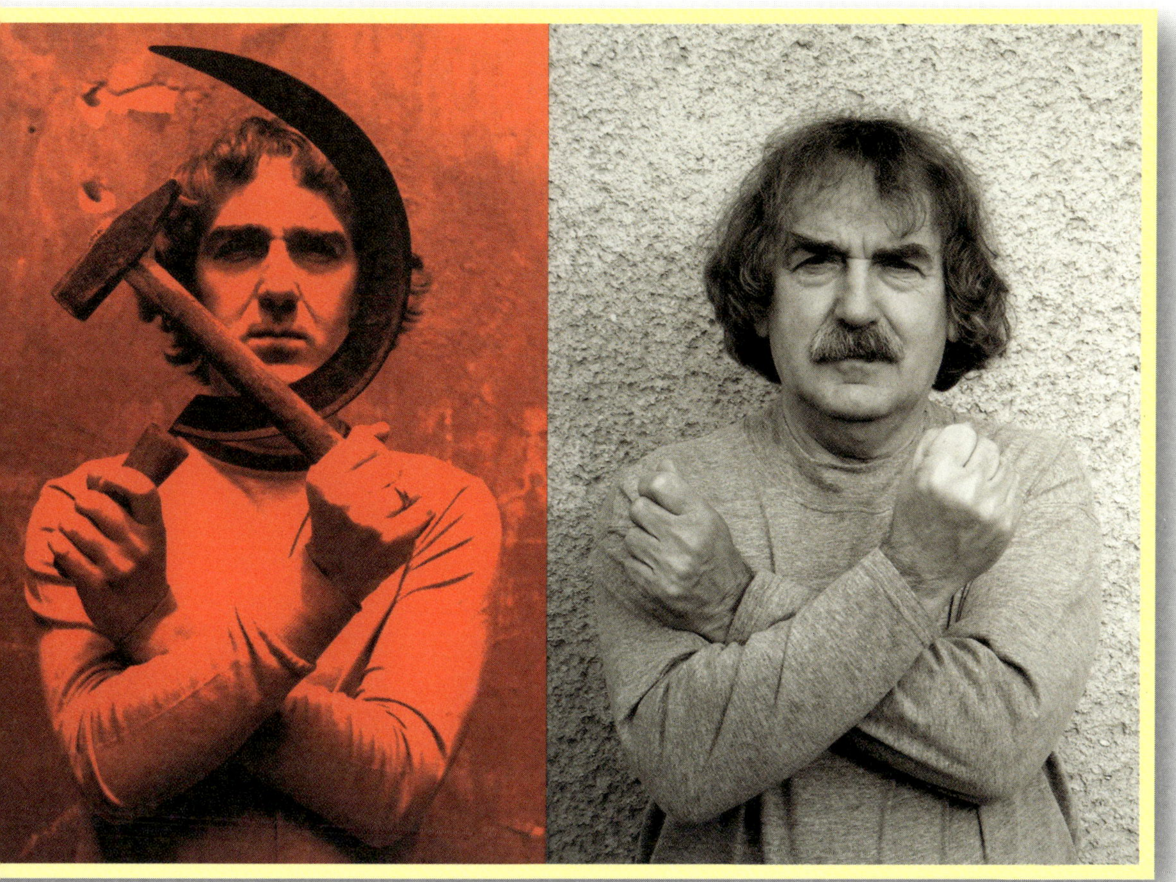

Fig. 26

Michele Zaggia

The film *Unpredicted Outcome* [*Figs.* 46 *ff.*] begins with the image of an eye; a spiral surrounds its corona. The spiral represents the game of Snakes and Ladders and, at the same time, Europe. While the eye symbolizes the human pretence of a direct and exhaustive knowledge of reality, the spiral (i.e. the eye's corona) alludes to the mirror, i.e. to the inevitably mediate and relative nature of knowledge, and to the human condition, perpetually exposed to contingency, risk and the unforeseen. At the beginning of the film, Europe (in the shape of Snakes and Ladders) is shown on a black background [*Figs.* 47]. This image expresses my idea about the relationship between 'necessity' and 'contingency', which, in brief, may be summarized as follows: people never deal with 'things', but always and only with 'meanings', or, rather, always and only with the necessary event of contingent meanings. The radical contingency of the meanings in my opinion makes it evident that every truth and every totalitarianism is just the expression of a wish for negative power (the ancient Greeks would call it *hybris*). In the film, Europe – just as in Snakes and Ladders – is divided into fields, representing the differences between each country, i.e. languages, cultures, religions, and ideologies that have developed over the centuries. The current processes of integration in Europe (which is inscribed in the general process of globalization) involves not only benefits, but also the threat that differences (culture, languages, hierarchy of values etc.) will rapidly be wiped out. If this happens, there is the risk of some form of totalitarianism, and hence of dictatorship. The tendency to wipe out the differences is fuelled not only by the market, but also by the unlimited power of technology, and by the unprecedented acceleration of the processes of transformation that this implies.

The rotation of the spiral refers to the consequences of the speed of the technological revolution. The rotation represents time. The faster the spiral turns, the more difficult it will be for Europeans to adapt their forms of life to the speed of change. In the centre of the spiral, I have drawn a small wheel that controls the direction (forward = future; backward = past) and the speed of rotation; certain situations happen, depending on how the wheel is manoeuvred; for example, it may happen that the thought of some philosophers contributes to preparing the cultural ground for the development of totalitarianism, or it may happen that the uncontrolled speed of change and the so-called 'End of History' cancel the individual or collective memory of what – for the best and for the worst – Europeans have been. I am not sure that I know who has the power to affect the wheel: from time to time this power has been granted to Need, to people's free will or to chance. On the basis of what I have written above concerning the relationship between need/necessity and contingency, I would venture to give the following answer: since we do not possess the Event, but only the interpretation of the meanings of what happens, it is our duty to be aware that they are changeable and, thus, we should not expect to enforce an absolute interpretation of them. Of course, this applies, first of all, to myself, because within the depths of the grotesque of the characters and situations that I love to portray, I exhibit a considerable amount of pessimistic nihilism. Thus, the 'optimistic' question which ends the film ('But is History really over?') is addressed to myself as well.

2007

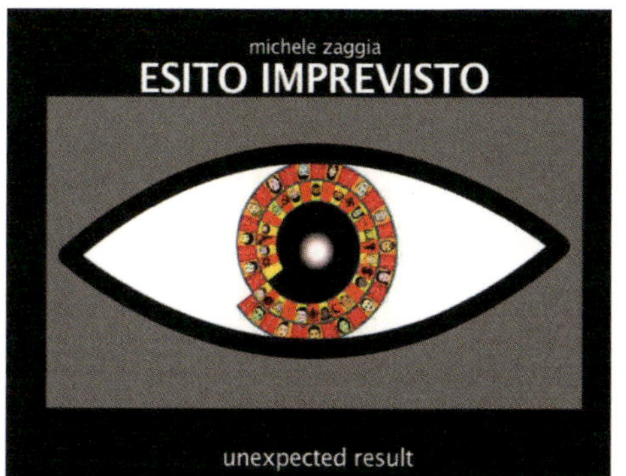

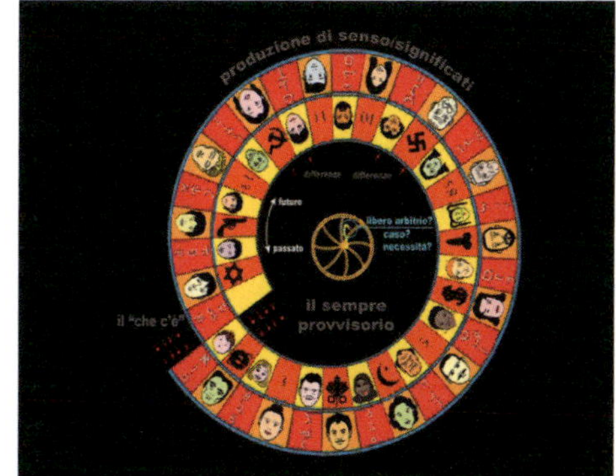

Figs. 46 and 47

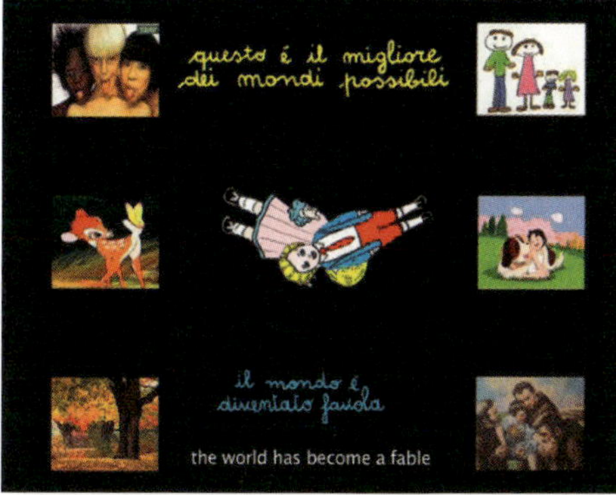

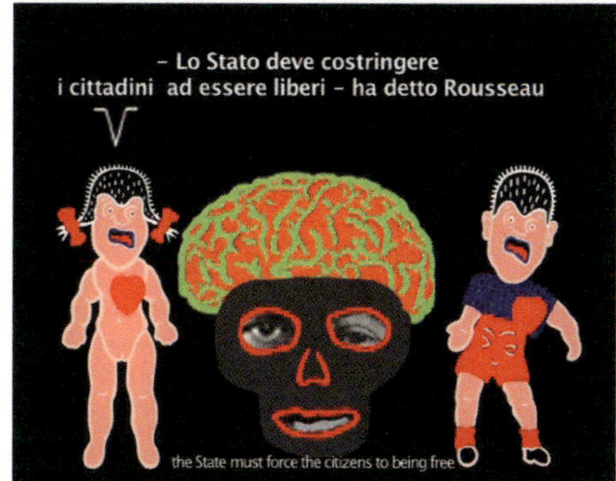

Figs. 48 and 49

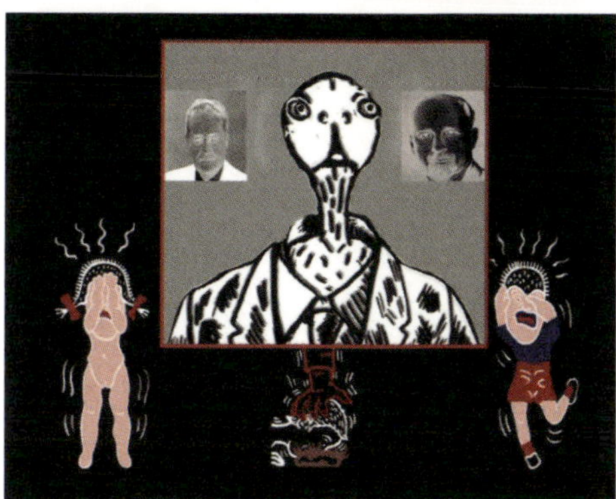

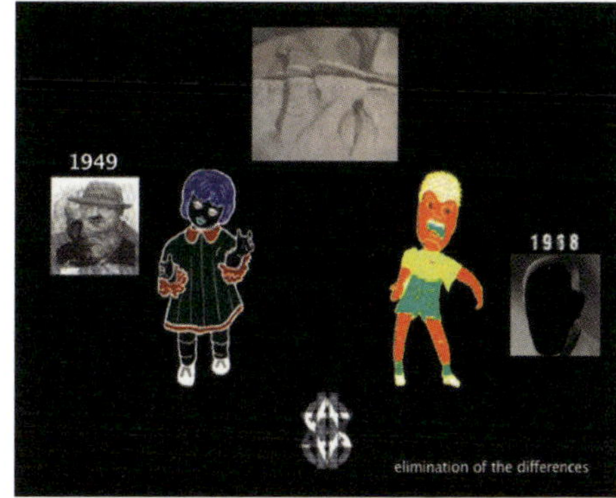

Figs. 50 and 51

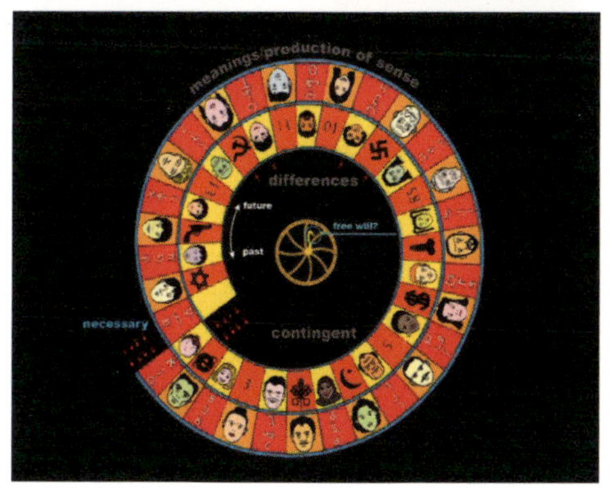

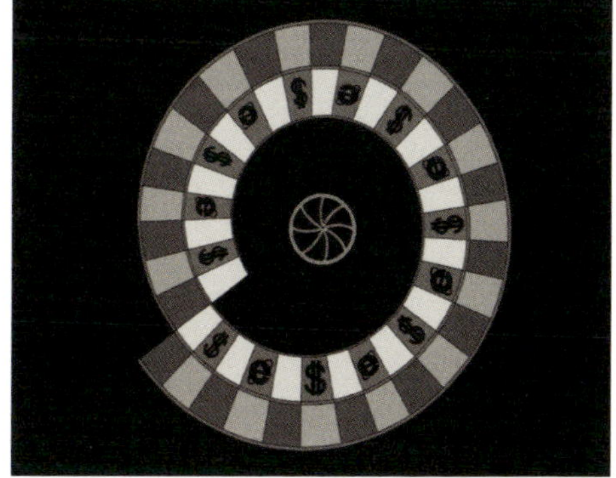

Figs. 52 and 53

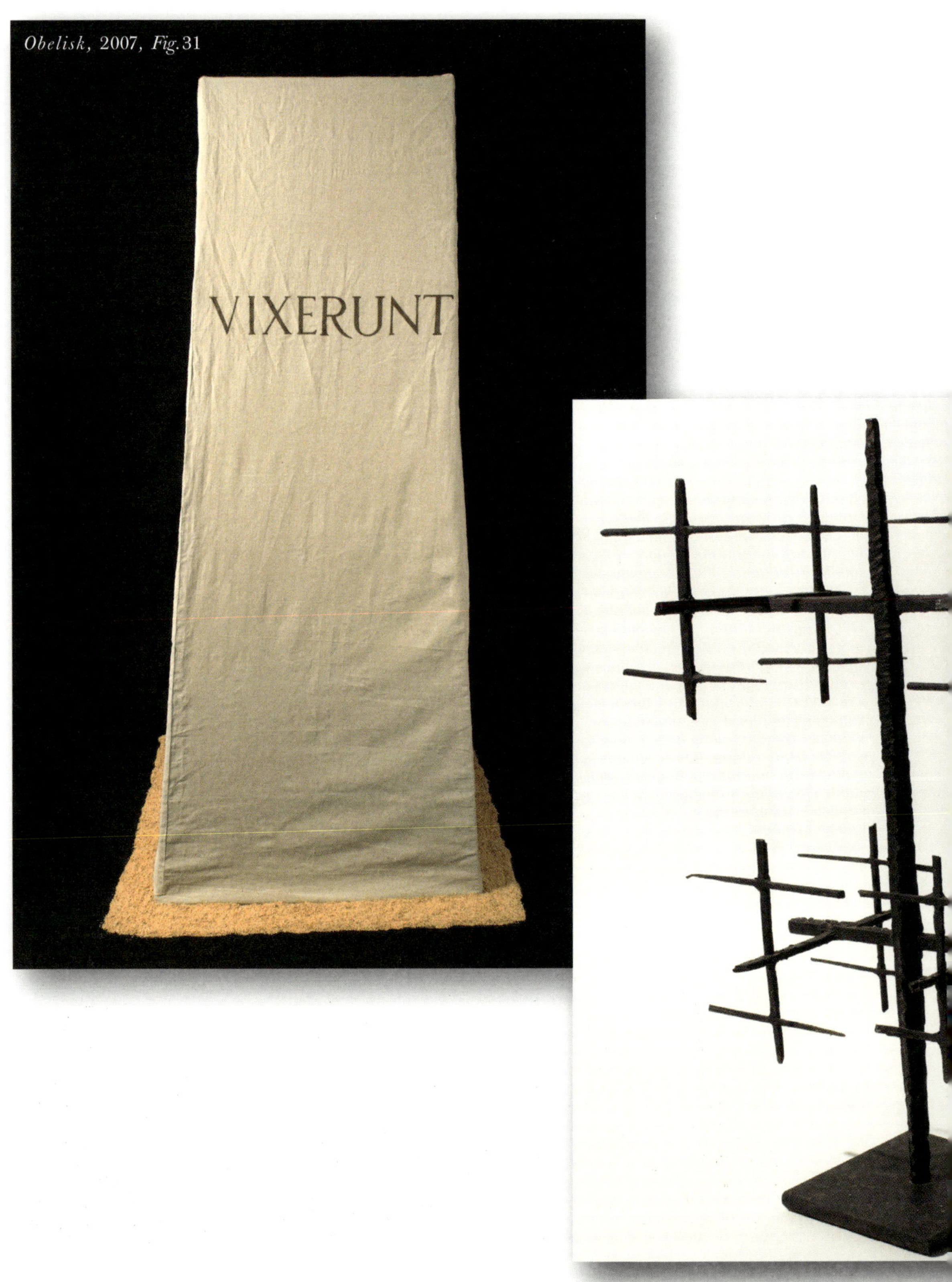
Obelisk, 2007, Fig. 31
VIXERUNT

My sculptures *Sickle and Hammer* of 1991 [*Fig.*8] and *Cross in Cross* of 1990 [*Fig.*9] came into existence as a reflection of a time when the dictatorship was gone, at first in Poland at the turn of the 1980s and the 1990s and then in the other countries of Central and Eastern Europe. Solidarity, the great social movement, initiated this process. Polish courage and spirit was supported by the Catholic Church, particularly Karol Wojtyła as Pope John Paul II. An individual was nobody in the dictatorship; however, the feeling of power as a community and the desire for a change, which the Polish people understood, led to the end of Communism in Poland. Artists were in the avantgarde of this move as they were feeling strongly the unbearable limitations. My small sculptures express the weakness of that ideology, but also the weight of the long-lasting system.

Obelisk was executed in 2007 as a result of my involvement in the project 'Overcoming Dictatorship' [*Fig.*31]. *Vixerunt* is a reflection on the brittleness of the seemingly great strength of authority. The dictatorship as an authority of the evil power can last a long time but it will always pass. Thus *Vixerunt* is a memento for all dictators and all dictatorships. The title refers to Cicero's words mentioned in the *Wielki słownik cytatów* (the so-called *Great Vocabulary of Quotations*) published by Literary Publishing Company in Kraków in 2007.

The form of the obelisk refers to the strength of the authority. The passing of this power is visible both in the unbleached linen and in the sawdust spilt at the base.

2007

Sickle and Hammer, 1991, *Fig.*8

Cross in Cross, 1990, *Fig.*9

Appendices

II Biographies of the Artists

The biographies have been compiled by Nellie Gilson (NG) and Antonia Grousdanidou (AG).

Zbyněk Benýšek

Czech Republic. Born in 1949
Lives and works in Prague

Benýšek grew up in Prostějov, Moravia. Graduating from the Secondary School of applied arts in Brno, he went on to study art at the University of F. Palacký Olomouc. After moving to Prague, he earned his living in several manual jobs, also working in the film industry and as a freelance musician. Persecuted as a signatory of *Charter 77*, experiencing interrogation and coercion to emigrate, in 1982 Benýšek moved to Vienna. Here he founded the émigré art review *Páternoster* and edited it for ten years, returning to Prague in 1992, where he has lived ever since. He is a member of both *Nové sdružení pražských malířů* (New Association of Prague's painters), and the Society of Czech writers. Besides composing new pieces of literature and working for television and broadcasting, he devotes much of his time to book graphics and the visual arts. As both an author and artist he is influenced by the philosophy of life of the underground. Originally identifying with Imaginative Realism, his works are increasingly marked by the blurring effects of fantasy and psychedelic forms.

Selected Solo Exhibitions

2008	Galerie Balbínka, Prague
2001	Galerie Platónská jeskyňka, Prague
2000	Museum des Prossnitzer Gebiets, Prossnitz
1999	Galerie antikvariátu v Kounické,
	Galerie Pamět, Prague
1998	Výstavní sály zámku, Prossnitz
1997	Galerie Alternatif, Prague
1995	Galerie K, Prague
1994	Galerie Paseka, Prague
	Galerie K, Prague
1993	Kabinet múz, Brno
1992	Stadtgalerie Fürstfeld, Austria
1990	Galerie Rapid, Prague
1988	Nachtasyl, Vienna
1986	Galerie Zur Brücke, Heidelberg
	Galerie Zur Bunten Kuh, Vienna
	Café Kafka, Frankfurt
1985	Galerie Töpfen, Frankfurt
	Galerie Dialog, Frankfurt
1984	Galerie Apostroph, Vienna
1978	Galerie v Náplavní, Prague
1968	SUPŠ, Brno

Selected Group Exhibitions

1997	Vyšehrad, Prague
1994	*New Union of Prague Artists*, Mánes, Prague;
	Stadtgalerie, Kutná Hora
1987	Ateliér K, Vienna
1982	*Czech Artists in Vienna*, Centre for International
	Culture, Vienna; Galerie Eulau 5, Berlin
1980	Zahradní výstava, Chýně (close to Prague)

Publications by the Artist

Vilémovo dilema, 2007
Pohádka o Filípkovi, 2006
Povídka o Rudolfkovi, 2004
Sonetten aus der Platonshöhle, 2004
Tma, 1999
Wir sind keine Mörder, 1999
Die Diagnose und andere Gedichte, 1998
'Pád labutě', *Páternoster*, no. 28, Prague, 1991
Valentýnka, 1987
Večírek u dr. Šimona, 1985
Výzkumní ústav, 1983
Langsatz, 1980
Die Verlesung des Morgensterns, 1976
Panoptikum, 1976
DramamarD, 1975
Die Pfarrerin, 1974
Karlsbad, 1973
Silvester, 1973
Der ausgetretene Pfad, 1972
Die Fliege, 1972
Frühlingsbegrüßung, 1972
Schůze první rozumné vlády, 1972
Vidění svatého muže, 1970
Notizen, 1967

Bibliography

— Various authors, *Hospody a pivo*, Academia, 1997
— Egon Bondy, 'Tři malíři', *Páternoster*, no. 1, 1983
— Eugen Brikcius, *Vyložený Zbyněk Benýšek*, 1999
— Eugen Brikcius, 'Tak pravil /a namaloval/ Zbyněk Benýšek', *Reflex*, 1995
— Eugen Brikcius, 'Vyložení umělci', *Inverze*, 1991
— Jiří Grusa, *Verfemte Dichter*, [Anthology of banned Czech authors], Bund-Verlag, Cologne, 1983
— Jiří Hůla, *Malíř Z. B. vytváří vlastní báje a mýty*, Lidové newspaper, 1999
— Vladimír Procházka, *Výstava Zbyňka Benýška*, Mělnicko, 1999
— Ivana Pustějovská, *Chci nahlédnout za roh reality*, MF Dnes, 1998
— Christa Rothmeier, *Die entzauberte Idylle*, Vienna, 2004
— Viktor Šlajchrt, *Básnické trasy a trapasy*, Pánu Bohu do oken, Respekt, 1999
— Vlasta Třešňák, 'Nové obrazy, Jack Rozparovač', *Páternoster*, no. 24-25, 1989
— Author Unknown, *Bez šilinku, v botách*, Interview, J.E. Fricem v Brně na Skleněné louce, 28 July 2005
— Author Unknown, *Z. B. v pražské galerii K*, Interiew, Lidové newspaper, 1995
— Author Unknown, *Páternoster* (Interview with founding members), ČR-Praha, 1992

Websites

www.benysek.wz.cz | www.galeriebenysek.wz.cz

—
NG

Zbigniew Czop

Poland. Born in 1943
Lives and works in Kraków

Born in Nowy Sącz, a town in the Lesser Poland Voivodeship in southern Poland, he studied painting and graphic arts in the Academy of Fine Arts in Kraków. His interests span from book and advertisement illustration through painting and sculpture to architecture and interior design. His greatest passion, though, remains copper engraving, an old technique that is rarely used by artists nowadays.

As a graphic artist he has had several exhibitions in Poland, Germany, Denmark and the Czech Republic. He is a board member of the Polish Cultural Foundation and has recently been commissioned to create a bookplate to commemorate the jubilee of Professor Aleksander Kravchuk (*1922), an esteemed politician.

Selected Exhibitions

1997   Krakowscy Twórcy w Antwerpii, Antwerp
1990   Instytut Kultury Polskiej, Prague
1983   The William Benton Museum of Art, Washington

—

AG

Mirela Dauceanu

Romania. Born in 1965
Lives and works in Bucharest

Born in Constanta, Romania, Dauceanu studied at the Academy of Arts in Bucharest. As well as being an accomplished stage designer, her art works have featured in group exhibitions internationally. Dauceanu's graphics, sculptures and installation are a testimony to the changes undergone by Romanian society. Her work presents a distinctive critique of consumerism which is also an important stimulus for her creative process. Dauceanu has lectured at the Faculty of Art History and Art Theory at the National University of Arts Bucharest since 2000.

Selected Stage Design and Installation

2007   Urban Space, Trixy Chechais Tribute, "Sertar" Project, Bucharest, Romania
2005   Domnişoara din Amherst, Foarte Mic Theatre, Bucharest; Maria Filotti Theatre, Brăila, Romania
2004   Homeopat experiment, Carturesti Gallery, Bucharest, Romania
2002   la douaspe' trecute fix, Oleg Danovski Theatre, Constanta, Romania
From Winter Story to The Dream of the Summer Night, Odeon Theatre, Bucharest, Romania
2001   Nijinsky Tribut, Odeon Theatre Bucharest, Romania
Woyzeck. Style Trilogy, Lucia Sturza Bulandra Theatre, Bucharest, Romania and International Sibiu Theatre Festival, Romania
FLYing. "Space Gallery", International Center for Contemporary Arts, Bucharest, Romania

Selected Group Exhibitions

2007   *Ambient Urban,* Meta Cultural Foundation, Sibiu, Romania
2005   *Brut 05,* German Cultural Centre, Sibiu, Romania
2001   *Process-Space Festival,* Rousse, Bulgaria
The Dream of My Life, Balkan Contemporary Art Biennial, National Gallery, Sofia, Bulgaria
Illusory Paradises, art and anthropology interdisciplinary symposium. Meta Foundation, Bucharest, Romania
2000   *In Full Dress,* Brukenthal Museum, Sibiu, Romania
1999   *Romanian Contemporary Art,* Munich, Germany
Mobile Studio, Eforie Gallery, Bucharest, Romania
1998   *Process-Space Festival,* Balchik, Bulgaria

Projetto 2000, Palazzo Brichera sio Gallery, Turin, Italy
Periferic 1, French Cultural Center, Iasi, Romania
Der Grüne Punkt, 35 Studio Eforie Gallery, Bucharest, Romania
1996   *Container 96: Art Across Oceans,* Copenhagen, Denmark
Una Finestra sull Est, San Fillipo Gallery, Turín, Italy
Spatial Art, World Trade Centre Plaza Bucharest, Romania
Cold Sun, ¾ Gallery, National Theatre Bucharest, Romania
1995   *Codex-/author's book,* Mogosoaia Cultural Center, Romania; Amsterdam, Netherlands
Neo-Traditionalism/Neo Avant-garda, Studio 35, Eforie Gallery, Bucharest, Romania
1994   *Essay for Compare Art,* National Museum, Bucharest, Romania
Impact. Art Festival '94, Kyoto, Japan
1993   *Impact. Art Festival '93,* Kyoto, Japan

Selected Bibliography

— Liviana Dan, *In Full Dress,* exh. cat., Brukenthal Museum, Sibiu (Romania), 2000
— Dimitar Grozdanov, *Process-Space Festival,* Balchik (Bulgaria), 1998
— Adrian Guta, *Romanian Contemporary Art,* place not known (Germany), 1999
— Erwin Kessler, *Spatial Art*, exh. cat., World Trade Centre Plaza, Bucharest (Romania), 1996
— David O'Halloran (et al.), Container 96 – *Art Across Oceans*, exh. cat., Copenhagen (Denmark), 1996

Works in Public Collections

Palazzo Bricherasio Gallery, Turin, Italy
Contemporary Art Museum, Bucharest, Romania

—

NG

Ulf Göpfert

Germany. Born in 1943
Lives and works in Dresden

Born in Freiberg, Saxony, as the son of Rolf Göpfert, a renowned architect, he completed a carpentry apprenticeship along with his studies for A levels, while receiving private lessons in painting and composition from 1960 to 1963. From 1963 to 1972 he earned his income as a furniture restorer in the castles and art collections of Weimar, Dresden and Potsdam (Sanssouci). From 1973 to 1990 he worked as a freelance furniture restorer in Dresden and was a member of the Association of Graphic Arts of the GDR. In 1983 he first encountered Pop Art in an exhibition in Leipzig, thus deciding to take up painting again; since 1986 his works have been shown in public exhibitions. Directly after the reunification he was head commissioner of culture and tourism for the city of Dresden (1990-1994), and has been working as a freelance painter since.

Selected Exhibitions

2008   *Ulf Göpfert – Metamorphosen,* Stadtarchiv Dresden

2005	Group Exhibition, Galerie Doris Kreiss, Dresden
1999	Bad Vilbel, Quellenhof
1998	Regierungspräsidium, Dresden
	Stadtarchiv, Haldensleben
1990	Führungsakademie Baden Württemberg, Karlsruhe
	Zentrale Dresdner Bank, Frankfurt a.M.
1989	Bezirkskunstausstellung, Dresden
1988	Galerie Comenius, Dresden (first exhibition)

Works in Public Collections and Public Art Works

2006	Carl Richard Montag, Stiftungen Bonn
2002	Stadthalle Burg
	(see www.stadt-burg.de/freizeit/stadthalle2/
	stadthalle_2.html)
2000	MDR Landesfunkhaus, Dresden
1998	Dresdner Bank, Dresden
1997	Dresdner Bank, Bischofswerda
1973	EB Kabelwerk, Meissen

Selected Bibliography

— Wolfgang Boesner and Yvonne Schwarzer (eds.), *Künstler. Werk. Material. 77 Künstlerwege,* Witten, 2004, 146-151
— Jördis Lademann, *Ulf Göpfert. Metamorphosen,* with an introduction by Jördis Lademann, exh. cat., Dresden, Stadtarchiv Dresden, 2007
— *Mehr als recht. Das Mandantenmagazin der Rechtsanwälte Dr. Holzhauser & Partner GbR,* 02/2002, 18

Website

www.goepfert-art.de

—

AG

Harald Hauswald

Germany. Born in 1954
Lives and works in Berlin

Born in Radebeul, near Dresden, he undertook an apprenticeship in photography from 1970 to 1972, taking his final examination in 1976. A year later he moved to East Berlin, where he worked in various jobs (including telegram messenger, restorer, photo-lab assistant and part-time photographer for the Stephanus Foundation). In 1989 he was admitted to the Association of Graphic Arts of the GDR, working as a freelance photographer since. His work has been exhibited in both Germanies, the USA, Switzerland, France, Italy and the Netherlands. He is also a founding member of Ostkreuz, a photographic agency, and has published photo-reportages in German and international magazines (including *GEO, Stern* and *Zeit Magazin*) and several books (some in collaboration).

Selected Solo Exhibitions

2008	*Jugendkulturen in der DDR,* Thüringer Fachhochschule für öffentliche Verwaltung, Gotha *Mythos Osteuropa,* Hoffmann-von-Fallersleben-Museum, Schloss Fallersleben, Wolfsburg
2007	*Neue Arbeiten (2000 - 2007),* imago fotokunst, Berlin *Gewendet. Vor und nach dem Mauerfall,* Freelens Galerie, Hamburg
2006	*Die dritte Halbzeit. Hooligans im Ost-Berlin der Wendezeit,* Galerie MFK, Berlin Berlin, Galerie Kunstblick, Berlin *Leben vor dem Mauerfall,* www.photography-now.com/institutions/I7454512.html?PHPSESSID=5c7b9fd04c1113617690420 88d7e25a7 Gedenkstätte Deutsche Teilung Marienborn, Marienborn
2005	*Ost-Berlin – Leben vor dem Mauerfall,* Abgeordnetenhaus, Berlin; Friedrich-Naumann-Stiftung, Potsdam-Babelsberg; Haus der Geschichte, Leipzig *Berliner Hooligans,* Vokuhila, Berlin *Berlin-Ost. Die andere Zeit einer Stadt,* Dokumentationszentrum Prora, Rügen *Vergessene Erinnerungen – Fotos von den Friedrichsstadtpassagen,* 1980, Galerie Aguirre, Berlin
2004	Imago Fotokunst, Berlin

Selected Group Exhibitions

2005	*Neueinstellung Ostkreuz – 17 Fotografische Positionen,* Ostkreuz group exhibition in collaboration with the Goethe Institut, Pfefferberg, Berlin and Galleria Grazia Neri, Milano *Utopie und Wirklichkeit – Ostdeutsche Fotografie 1956-1989,* Willy-Brandt-Haus, Berlin and Forum für Fotografie, Cologne
2002	*Augenblicke-Augenzeugen. Bilder aus Berlin,* Ostkreuz travelling exhibition in collaboration with the Goethe Institute, Gorkij Literaturmuseum, Nischnij Nowgorod
1999	*Östlich von Eden. Von der DDR nach Deutschland 1974-1999,* Ostkreuz group exhibition, Postfuhramt Berlin
1993	*Aufbruch nach Deutschland,* Deutsches Historisches Museum, Ostkreuz group exhibition, Berlin

Published Photographs (selection)

— Harald Hauswald, *Alexanderplatz. Fotografische und literarische Erinnerungen,* Berlin, 2007
— Harald Hauswald/Lutz Rathenow, *Gewendet. Vor und nach dem Mauerfall.* Fotos und Texte aus dem Osten, Berlin, 2006
— Harald Hauswald/Lutz Rathenow, *Ost-Berlin. Leben vor dem Mauerfall. Life before the wall fell* (text in German and English), Berlin, 2005 (2nd edition 2005, 3rd edition 2006)
— Harald Hauswald, *Seitenwechsel. Fotografien 1979-1999,* Berlin, 1999
— Volker Handloik, Harald Hauswald and others (eds.), *Die DDR wird 50. Texte und Fotografien,* Berlin: Aufbau-Verlag, 1998 (= Fünfzig Jahre DDR. Texte und Fotografien, Berlin, 1999, 2nd edition)
— Harald Hauswald/Lutz Rathenow, *Berlin-Ost. Die andere Seite einer Stadt,* Berlin, 1990
— Harald Hauswald and Lutz Rathenow, *Ostberlin. Die andere Seite einer Stadt in Texten und Bildern,* Munich, 1987

Selected Bibliography

— Frank Döbert, 'Glänzende Fotos, spitze Feder',
  Ostthüringer Zeitung, 31 Jan. 2007
— Christian Dorn, 'Schwarzweiss in Zwischentönen',
  Melodie und Rhythmus, no. 1, 2007, 78-80
— Christian Dorn, 'Leben vor dem Mauerfall',
  Melodie und Rhythmus, no. 2, 2007, 84-86
— Gabriele Eckart, Review of Harald Hauswald/Lutz
  Rathenow, *Ost-Berlin. Leben for dem Mauerfall. Life
  before the wall fell* (text in German and English),
  Berlin: Jaron Verlag, 2005, Glossen, no. 23, 2006
  (www.dickinson.edu/departments/germn/glossen/
  heft23/eckart.html)
— Barbara Glasser, 'Bilder erzählen kleine Geschichten',
  Thüringische Landeszeitung, 8 Feb. 2007
— Stefanie Grießbach, 'Lebensbilder',
  Ostthüringische Zeitung, 12 Feb. 2007
— Ralph Grüneberger, 'DDR-Fotografien der 70er und
  80er heute gesehen', *Leipzigs Neue,* 23 Dec. 2005
— Astrid Kuhlmey, 'Gewendet [review of the book by
  Hauswald' and Rathenow]', *Brennpunkt,* no. 1, 2007, 25
— Katharina Lenski, 'Ewige DDR', *Deutschland Archiv,*
  no. 3, 2007, 401-403
— Giovanni di Lorenzo, 'Bevor alles gleich war',
  Zeitmagazin, no. 46, 8 Nov. 2007, 42-51
— Ulrike Merkel, 'Ewige DDR', *Ostthüringer Zeitung,*
  23 Feb. 2007
— Chaim Noll, 'Berlin einst und jetzt',
  Neues Deutschland, 1 March 2007
— Lutz Rathenow, 'Dissident am Auslöser',
  Rheinischer Merkur, no. 40, 2007
— Ingeborg Ruthe, 'Ein Narbengesicht, das östlichste,
  ehrlichste der Stadt', *Berliner Zeitung,* 16 Oct. 2007
— Karim Saab, 'Mit beseeltem Blick',
  Die Märkische, 4/5 Feb. 2006

Awards

2006   Einheitsreis - Bürgerpreis zur Deutschen Einheit,
        Bundeszentrale für politische Bildung
1997   Order of Merit of the Federal Republic of Germany

Website

www.harald-hauswald.de

—
AG

Silvestro Lodi

Italy. Born in 1947
Lives and works in Venice

Silvestro Lodi graduated from the Academy of Fine Art
Venice in 1969 and has exhibited his work internationally.
Merging painting with sculpture, Lodi's mixed media
installations draw on the anthropology of historical and
contemporary life. Influenced by Giorgio de Chirico as well
as Duchamp and Dada, self-proclaimed 'social artist' Lodi
aims for a 'complete liberty of imagination.' For many
years he has stood as an elected member of the Cultural
Commission for the Fondazione Bevilacqua La Masa in
Venice. In 1992, Lodi co-founded *Qnst,* the journal of
art and design. Since the 1970s, he has held teaching
roles at prestigious art institutions, and since 1999, taught
at the University of Venice.

Selected Solo Exhibitions

2006   *Vibrazioni,* Galleria l'Occhio, Venice
2004   *Carte d'acqua,* Galleria Cartavenezia, Venice
        Materia, Associazione culturale 'La Parada',Brescia
2003   *Herenowhere,* Galleria della Scuola
        Internazionale di Grafica, Venice
1999   *Partiture,* Studio Lattuada, Milan
1997   *A. Z.,* Santa Maria di Feletto, Treviso
        Sopraffazioni, Treffpunkt zur Documenta X,
        Kassel, Germany
1996   *Senza Titolo,* Galleria Odradek, Venice
1995   *Geografie della storia,* Studio Tommaseo,
        Trieste; Studio Delise, Portogruaro; Studio
        Gennai, Pisa; G.Licandro Galerie, Vienna, Austria
1992   *Liriche Ossessioni,* Galleria Sintesi, Treviso
1991   *Remoto assente,* Galleria Il Traghetto, Venice
        Realismi della memoria, Studio Tommaseo, Trieste
1989   *Presente remoto,* Galleria Unimedia, Genoa
1984   Galleria Il Traghetto, Venice
1981   *Immagine/Immaginario,* Studio Toni De Rossi,
        Verona
1978   Galleria Il Traghetto, Venice
        Galleria della Fondazione Bevilacqua La Masa,
        Venice
        Galleria Palmieri, Milan
1977   *Arcana,* Museo Correr, Ala Napoleonica, Venice
1976   *Tempi di Lodi,* Galleria Il Traghetto,Venice
        Galleria San Domenico, Mantova
        Galleria Incontro Arti Visive, Venice
1974   Galleria Il Traghetto 2, Venice

Selected Group Exhibitions

2004   *Tre pareti e una scala-Trent'anni di attività
        1974-2004,* Studio Tommaseo, Trieste
1999   *Argento Vivo,* Studio Tommaseo, Trieste
        Comunicazione 2000, Italienisch- Österreichisches
        Austauschprojekt, Istituto Italiano di Cultura,
        Vienna, Austria
1998   *Lautlos,* Universität Klagenfurt, Institut für
        Allgemeine und Vergleichende Literaturwissen
        schaft, Klagenfurt, Austria
1997   *Dopo Tiepolo,* Fondazione Bevilacqua La Masa,
        Venice
1996   *Nuova Insularità,* Galleria Internazionale d'Arte
        Moderna, Ca' Pesaro, Venice
        La Pittura Colta in Italia – Anacronisti, Abbazia
        Olivetana, Rodengo Saiano, Brescia
1995   *Presenze in Pinacoteca,* Pinacoteca d'arte
        moderna, Castello Orsini Colonna, Avezzano
1994   *Materiali e Linguaggi,* AL-EXPO, Alessandria
        Insulae. L'arte dell'esilio, Studio Gennai, Pisa
        A-ISM Le universali individualità dell'arte, Istituto
        Italiano di Cultura e A-ISM, G. Licandro Galerie,
        Vienna, Austria
1993   *Pixellated Pixel,* La Biennale di Venezia – XLV
        Esposizione Internazionale d'Arte, Punti Cardinali
        dell'Arte, Casino Container, Venice
        Insulae & Insulae, La Biennale di Venezia – XLV
        Esposizione Internazionale d'Arte, Ca' Giustinian,
        Venice
1992   *Giuseppe Mazzariol, 50 artisti a Venezia,*
        Fondazione Scientifica Querini Stampalia, Venice
1991   *10,20,200,* Studio Tommaseo, Trieste
        Pentagonale Plus, Richard Demarco Gallery,

Edinburgh, Scotland
1989   *L'occhio della galleria,*
Galleria Bevilacqua La Masa, Venice
1988   *Clinamina,* Studio Tommaseo, Trieste
1986   *Sguardi a Nord Est,* Palazzo dei Diamanti, Ferrara
Aperto, Studio Tommaseo, Trieste Visionaria
Venezia, Galleria Unimedia, Genoa
Se Noè vizia Arianna, Arianna sevizia Noè,
Galleria Avida Dollars, Milan
1985   *Aspetti della nuova pittura a Venezia,* S.I.M.A.,
Venice
1984   *Sodobni Beneski Umetniki,* Moderna Galerija,
Lubiana, Yugoslavia
Segni Paralleli, Ca'Vendramin Calergi, Venice
Omaggio al Pordenone, Galleria Sagittaria,
Pordenone
Intergrafik, Berlin, Germany
1982   *la Biennale internazionale della Grafica,* Riva del
Garda, Trento, Italy
Proiezioni: Arte nel Veneto 70/80, Museo di
Ca'Pesaro e Fondazione Bevilacqua La Masa,
Venice
1981   *Triennale Europea dell'Incisione,* Palazzo dei
congressi, Grado
1980   VII Rassegna Internazionale della Grafica
Contemporanea, Galleria d'Arte Moderna e
Contemporanea, Forlì
1979   *Premio Campigna,* Campigna e Forlì
1977   *Arcana,* Museo Correr, Ala Napoleonica, Venice
Tendances et Recherches, Maison de Beaux Arts
de France, Paris
1976   *La Biennale di Venezia.* XXXVII Esposizione
Internazionale d'Arte, Padiglione sviz zero, Venice

Selected Publications by the Artist

— 'Intervista', *In Contrattempo La Pittura malgrado
tutto,* Milan, 2007
— 'Il limite dell'arte, relazione al Congresso
Internazionale', *Arte e scrittura nelle situazioni limite,*
Zagreb, 1995
— 'Solo sotto le stelle' (colloquio con D. Del Giudice),
Risk arte oggi, no. 17, 1995, Milan, 1995
— 'Il polo del contemporaneo', *Qnst,* no. 6, Venice, 1994
— 'Un gentilhomme de mauvais goût', *Risk arte oggi,*
no. 15, 1994, Milan, 1994
— 'Arte punto zero', *Qnst,* no. 4, Venice, 1993
— 'Insulae & Insulae', *Qnst,* no. 3, Venice, 1993
— 'Forme del ri-fare', *Qnst,* no. 0, Venice, 1992
— *Valenze teoriche del fare-Verso una ecologia
dell'insegnamento,* Venice, 1990
— Silvestro Lodi, 'L'artista tra professione e vendetta',
Creativa, no. 8, Geneva, 1986

Bibliography

— L. M. Barbero, *Emblemi d'Arte,*
da Boccioni a Tancredi, Milan, 1999
— E. Bargiacchi, 'Le vicende artistiche significative del
nuovo corso artistico', *Forma senza forma,*
Modena and Pisa, 1982, 109?!
— Christian Boltanski, *Liste des artistes ayant participé
à la Biennale de Venise 1895-1995,* Paris, 1995
— D. C. Cadoresi, 'Silvestro Lodi', *Il paesaggio del mito
nell'arte contemporanea,* San Daniele del Friuli
(Udine), 1988
— G. Carbi, *Tre pareti e una scala,* Trieste, 2004
— F. De Santi, *Segni Paralleli,*
Stampa Istituto Artigianelli, Brescia, 1984
— Massimo Donà, 'Remembrance of Forgotten Music.
The Impersonality of "Truth" in the Paintings of
Silvestro Lodi', Silvestro Lodi, *Vibrazoni,* exh. cat.,
Vanezia, Galleria d'Arte l'Occhio, 2006, no page
— Massimo Donà, 'Arcanum Materiae', *Art in Italy,*
no. 6, 1995 (Adriano Parise Editore, Verona), 6-10
— Massimo Donà, 'Distanti Geo-grafie', *Silvestro Lodi,
Geografie della Storia,* Trieste, 1995
— Carlo Gentili, *Immagine/Immaginario,* Venice, 1980
— Laura Maggi, *Scatole d'artista,*
Casa Vogue, no. 230, Milan, 1991
— D. Marangon, 'Indici di storia', *Aspetti della ricerca
artistica a Palermo e Venezia,* Palermo, Venice, 1987
— E. Pontiggia, 'Araldica metafisica', *Remoto Assente,*
Venice, 1991
— Enzo Santese, *Artevisione,* Slovenia, 2003
— Enzo Santese, 'Lodi', *Juliet,* no. 34, 1987, 59
— F. Solmi, *Omaggio al Pordenone,* Pordenone, 1984
— T. Toniato, *Dizionario visivo delle cose del mondo,*
Kassel, 2002
— T. Toniato, 'Silvestro Lodi. Arte a Venezia-immagini di
ieri e di oggi', *Dopo Tiepolo,* Milan, 1997
— T. Toniato, *Modernità allo specchio,* Arte a Venezia
1860-1960, Venice, 1995

Works in Public Collections

— Galleria d'Arte Moderna 'ca' pesaro, Venice
— Museo Bargellini, Piere di Cento, Bologna
— Galleria d'Arte Moderna d'Avezzano

—
NG

Vlad Nancă

*Born in 1979
Lives and works in Bucharest*

Artist and curator Nancă studied photography and video
at the University of Arts in Bucharest. Drawing on the
environment and influence of Bucharest life, he documents
urbanity through his photography. Actively involved in
the progression of the city art scene, he also hosts 'home
galleries', and curates exhibitions, giving local artists a
platform to show their work. Nancă's varying projects
employ political and cultural symbols, often using word-
play to evoke nostalgia and referencing Romania's recent
history and current social climate.

Selected Solo Exhibitions

2007   *Happy Sunday,* installation, performance,
Work-of-the-month at the Contemporary Art
Museum, Bucharest
Galeria Noua Home Gallery, Galeria Noua,
Bucharest
Boulevard Renault 12, French Institute, Bucharest
Dream of Bucharest, Akademie Schloss Solitude,
Stuttgart
2005   *Ups and Downs,* H'art Gallery, Bucharest
Errorism, DSBA Gallery, Bucharest
Terrorism, Sex Trade Gallery, Bucharest
2003   *Vlad Nancă lives and works in Romania,*
2020 Home Gallery, Bucharest
Down to Earth, CIRKUS Gallery, SKC, Belgrade,

Framing Huesca, public art project and exhibition, Huesca, Spain

2001   *Swing Me,* International Center for Contemporary Arts, Bucharest

Selected Group Exhibitions

2008   *Sconfini, CONTRO IGNOTI,* Spazio Publico Arte Contemporanea, Buttrio, Italy
2007   *Social Cooking,* NGBK, Berlin
Art For Fun, Casal Solleric, Palma de Mallorca
Der Prozess, Prague Biennale 3, Prague
Editing Project, Rome
Ideal Urbanities, Akademie Schloss Solitude, Stuttgart
2006   *We Are The Artists: Mixed Pickels 2,* K3, Zurich
Playing With Terrorism, Künstlerverein Malkasten, Düsseldorf
Polish Year in Madagascar, Antananarivo, Madagascar; Atlas Stzuki, Łódź
Black Box, House of Arts, Brno, Czech Republic
2005   *We Are The Artists: Mixed Pickels 1,* K3, Zurich, Switzerland
Playing with Terrorism, MASC Foundation, Vienna
Fake, ATA Contemporary Art Center, Plovdiv, Bulgaria
On Difference #1, Kunstverein Stuttgart
2004   *Romanian Artists (And Not Only) Love Ceauşescu's Palace?!,* Contemporary Art Museum, Bucharest
2003   *Preview,* Kalinderu Medialab, Contemporary Art Museum, Bucharest

Other Projects

2006   *Curating of Wait ...* (Marwan Anbaky, Alina Andrei, Tudor Ene, Tudor Prisacariu, Lucian Stan), photography exhibition, Galeria Noua, Bucharest
2005   *± 15 Years/2020,* Galeria Noua, Bucharest
2004   *I Do Not Know What Union I Want to Belong to Anymore,* object inserted in *Idea,* an arts and society magazine, Cluj, Romania
2004   *I Do Not Know What Union I Want to Belong to Anymore,* billboard poster project, Bratislava, Slovakia
2004   *Revolution Brand,* performance at April Meetings, Belgrade, Serbia

Selected Bibliography

— Vlad Nancă with text by Jean-Baptiste Joly, *Dream of Bucharest,* exh. cat, Akademie Schloss Solitude, Stuttgart, May 2007
— Irina Cios, Aurora Király (et al.), *Photography in Contemporary Art: Trends in Romania After 1989,* Galeria Nouă, Editura Unarte, Bucharest, 2006
— Cosmin Costinas, 'New Fetishisms: A New Generation in Romanian Contemporary Art', *Umelec,* Bucharest, 3/2004

Awards

Several Scholarships in the European Artist-In-Residence-Programme (MAP programme, Paris 2002; quartier21, Vienna 2005 and Akademie Schloss Solitude, Stuttgart 2006)

Website and Blog

www.vladnanca.blogspot.com · www.bukresh.blogspot.com

—
NG

Sándor Pinczehelyi

Born in 1946, Szigetvár, Hungary
Lives and works in Pécs, Hungary

Pinczehelyi graduated from the Teacher's Training College in Pécs in 1970. Between 1977 and 1999 he was the director of the Pécs Art City Gallery. He organized over 500 exhibitions in Hungary and abroad, including numerous graphic and poster shows of internationally renowned artists. In 2000 he became director of the Visual Arts Faculty of the University in Pécs.
His interest turned to the political symbols of Hungary (sickle and hammer, star, cobblestone) in the early 1970s, when with a strong ironical undertone he lifted these then current symbols into his art. In the 1980s his visual actions using different techniques (graphics, painting, photo, installation, video) centred around the national tricolor of red-white-green. In 1988 he exhibited in the Hungarian Pavilion of the Venice Biennale.
Several museums in Hungary and Europe include his works in their collection. His art is recognized world wide.

Solo Exhibitions

2007   *Reprintek és tárgyak,* Centrális Galéria, Budapest
2006   *Spájz,* Pécsi Galéria, Pécs,
Látogatás, Galéria umenia, Nové Zámky
2005   *Fotómunkák / Photoworks 1972-1980,* Vintage Galéria, Budapest
2003   *Foszlánymaradvány,* Csikász Galéria, Veszprém
Pertu No. 5, Galéria mesta Bratislavy, Bratislava (Julius Kollerrel)
2002   *Aller-Retour Lyon-Pécs aux Subsistances,* Musée d'Art Contemporain, Lyon
Már megint, Budapest Galéria Kiállítóháza, Budapest
2001   *"In Anfürungszeichen",* Galerie der Stadt Fellbach, Germany
1999   Fővárosi Képtár – Kiscelli Múzeum, Budapest
1998   *Ismétlések,* Múzeum Galéria, Pécs
1996   *Átfestések,* Szent István Király Múzeum, Székesfehérvár
1994   *A vonat elment,* Fészek Galéria, Budapest
1989   *Konsthall,* Lund (Bukta Imrével és Samu Gézával)
1988   *XLIII La Biennale di Venezia,* Magyar Pavilon, Venezia (Bukta Imrével és Samu Gézával)
1987   Neue Galerie am Landesmuseum Joanneum, Graz
Musée Saint Pierre Art Contemporain, Lyon
1986   Ernst Múzeum, Budapest
Pécsi Galéria, Pécs
Galleri Gamlebyen, Fredrikstad
1983   Csók István Képtár, Székesfehérvár
Galeria Rzezby, Warszawa
1982   Stúdió Galéria, Budapest
1980   Taidemuseo, Lahti
1974   Janus Pannonius Múzeum, Pécs

Works in Public Collections (selection)

— Magyar Nemzeti Galéria, Budapest
— Ludwig Múzeum / Kortárs Művészeti Múzeum, Budapest
— Janus Pannonius Múzeum, Pécs
— Szent István Király Múzeum, Székesfehérvár
— Szombathelyi Képtár, Szombathely
— Miskolci Galéria – Városi Művészeti Múzeum, Miskolc
— Városi Művészeti Múzeum, Győr
— Paksi Képtár, Paks
— Museum Moderner Kunst / Stiftung Ludwig, Vienna
— Neue Galerie am Landesmuseum Joanneum, Graz
— Museum für Kunsthandwerk, Frankfurt am Main
— Neue Galerie, Sammlung Ludwig, Aachen
— Museum für Kunst und Gewerbe, Hamburg
— Museum of Art, Tel-Aviv
— Musée d'Art Contemporain, Lyon
— Musée d'Art Moderne, Saint Etienne
— Taidemuseo, Lahti
— Museum Fredrikstad
— GGG Gallery, Tokyo
— Národni Galeria, Prague
— Moravská Galeria, Brno
— Muzeum umeni, Olomouc
— Galéria umenia, Nové Zámky
— Muzej Savremene Umjetnosti, Sarajevo
— Muzeum Plakatu, Warsaw
— Muzeum Narodowe, Wrocław
— Muzeum Narodowe, Szczecin
— Muzeum Sztuki, Łódź

Awards

2004   Honoured artist of the Hungarian Republic
1989   Mihály Munkácsy Award, Budapest
1987   Award of the National Graphic Birennial, Miskolc
1984   Prize at the 6th Norwegian Print Biennial, Fredrikstad
1983   Award of the National Graphic Birennial, Miskolc
1980   Studio Prize, Budapest

Bibliography

— T. Aknai, *Sándor Pinczehelyi,* exh. cat., Pécs, 1977
— Jean Baudrillard, *Sándor Pinczehelyi,* exh. cat., Lyon, 1987
— L. Beke, *Sándor Pinczehelyi,* exh. cat., Pécs, 1974
— John Grande, *Balance. Art and Nature,* Montreal, 1994
— Péter György, 'Hungarian Marginal Art in the Late Period of State Socialism', Ales Erjavec (ed.), *Postmodernism and the Postsocialist Condition,* Berkeley, 2003, 175-207
— Lóránd Hegyi, *Pinczehelyi,* exh. cat., Pécs, 1995
— Lóránd Hegyi, *Utak az avantgárdból,* Pécs, 1989
— Lóránd Hegyi, *Sándor Pinczehelyi's Emblematic Art,* exh. cat., Venice, 1988
— Janus Pannonius Museum (ed.), *Pinczehelyi: Ismetlesek = Pinczehelyi: Repetitions, Pécs,* 1998
— K. Keserü, L. Hegyi, M. Kovalovsky, J. Frank, Gy Kemény Gy, *Sándor Pinczehelyi,* exh. cat., Fehérgyarmat, 1984
— K. Keserü, *Sándor Pinczehelyi,* exh. cat., Székesfehérvár, 1983
— Miklós Kovalovszky, Gy Várkonyi, *Már megint/And Again,* exh. cat., Budapest, 2002
— Miklós Kovalovszky, *Tyúkanyó meséi 15/Make up. Mother Hen's Tales 15,* exh. cat., Székesfehérvár, 1996
— Mária Orisková, *Dvojhlasné dejiny umenia,* Bratislava, 2002
— *Sándor Pinczehelyi. Graphic Design,* exh. cat., Pécs, 2002
— *Sándor Pinczehelyi's Emblematic Art,* exh. cat., Venice, 1988
— Piotr Piotrowski, *Awantgarda w cieniu Jaty,* Poznan, 2005, 301-303
— Steven Rand and Heather Kouris (eds.), *On Cultural Influence,* Apexart, 2006
— Gy Várkonyi, *Ismétlések/Repetitions,* exh. cat., Pécs, 1998

———
AG

Michele Zaggia

Italy. Born in 1946
Lives and works in Venice

After reveiving a degree in Philosophy at Ca'Foscari University, Venice, Zaggia taught Philosophy until his retirement in 2002. More recently he has worked with the Fine Arts Academy of Brera, giving theoretical and practical lessons on the Graphic novel, his particular area of interest. Alongside teaching, he established two cultural associations, Koinos and Nemus, and collaborated with others such as Guggenheim Public, for which he held lectures, seminars and wrote texts. Today he works as a graphic and comic strip artist for Rivista orale di filosfia, arti e scienze, a multimedia magazine. Together with Silvestro Lodi he contributed to the Joseph Beuys memorial performance e-natura. Percorrerre i confini at the Venice Biennale in 2007.

Group Exhibitions

2007   *Usitate catastrofi,* il Centro Culturale Candiani di Venice
        E-Natura and Ombre. Joseph Beuys. Defense of Nature. The Living Sculpture, Kassel 1977-Venice 2007, 52nd Biennale Venice

Selected Publications by the Artist

2006   Michele Zaggia, 'Usitate catastrofi', *Rivista rale di filosofie, arte e scienze,* Venice, 2006
2006   Michele Zaggia, 'Maurizio Pellegrin', Alice Rubbini (ed.) *Writings on Maurizio Pellegrin.1980-2006,* Milano, 2006, 144-147
2005   Michele Zaggia, 'Sul significato di "rischio"', Associazione culturale Nemus (ed.), *Il rischio e l'anima dell'Occidente,* Venice, 2005, 15-16
2003   Michele Zaggia (*et al.*), *Entretiens,* Galleria Michela Rizzo associazione culturale Synolon, September 2003
2001   Michele Zaggia, 'Logos e immagine', *Metamorfosi del logos,* vol. 1/3, Venice, 2001, 27-33

Work in Progress

A graphic novel set in seventeenth-century Venice. A story
in which the philosophers Spinoza and Leibniz are caught
up in some mysterious murders.

—
NG

Aleksander Marek Zyśko

Poland. Born in 1960
Lives and works in Wrocław

He grew up in Turobin (East Poland), lives in Jeszkowice
near Wrocław and works at the Academy of Fine Arts in
Wrocław.
He sculpts, draws and takes artistic photographs. In his
works, he most often presents the passage of time, the
condition of contemporary life and its relation to nature. In
the years of the decline of Communism, during his studies
at the secondary artistic school in Lublin, he co-organ-
ized a group of young people, who were opponents of the
Communist dictatorship.

Solo Exhibitions

2005   Gallery of the Academy of Fine Arts, Wrocław
2003   Office of Artistic Exhibitions, Lublin
2002   Orońsko, Centre of Polish Sculpture
2001   Gallery Skalna, Strzelin
1995   Museum of the Medal Engraving Art, Wrocław
1992   Gallery Wrocław

Selected Group Exhibitions

2007   Saloniki, Greece
2007   Colorado Springs, USA
2006   National Museum Poland, Wrocław
        Düsseldorf
2005   Museum of the Archdiocese Poland, Wrocław
        Museum of Architecture Poland, Wrocław
1998   Uherskie Chradiszcze, Czech Republic
1990   *'Incentive' Poland*, Warsaw
1989   *Toruń* (exhibition of the best diploma in 1988-89),
        Academy of Fine Arts, Wrocław
1987   Mons, Belgium

Awards and Prizes

2005   Distinction of ZPAP (The Association of Polish
        Artists)
2004   Niemcza competition (with a sculpture of
        St. Jadwiga), Second prize

Bibliography

— Author unknown, n.t., *Dyskurs,* no. 4, 2006
— Author unknown, 'Passing', *Annales UMCS Lublin,*
   vol. 60, 2006

—
AG

List of Illustrations

I would like to thank all those who have kindly given permission to reproduce the illustrations listed below. Every effort has been made to trace the copyright owners of works reproduced. The publishers apologize for any omissions that my inadvertantly have been made. Measurements are given in centimetres, height before width before depth unless otherwise stated.

1   Workshop 2 in Wałbrzych (Poland), 30 March to 1 April 2007, photo Barbara Lubich

2   Workshop 6 in Trent (Italy), 9 to 10 May 2008, photo Silvestro Lodi

3   Vlad Nancă showing us Bucharest, Workshop 5 in Bucharest (Romania), 7 to 9 Dec. 2007, photo Gert Röhrborn

4   Workshop 5 in Bucharest (Romania), 7 to 9 Dec. 2007, photo Barbara Lubich

5   Workshop 2 in Wałbrzych (Poland), 30 March to 1 April 2007, photo Silvestro Lodi

6   Vlad Nancă, *Original Adidas*, 2003, sculpture (mixed media), sizes vary, the artist's collection, photo Vlad Nancă © Vlad Nancă

7   Zbyněk Benýšek, *Saint Sebastian*, 1993, oil on canvas, 105 x 150, the artist's collection, photo Luke Unsworth © Zbyněk Benýšek

8   Aleksander Zyśko, *Sickle and Hammer*, 1991, bronze sculpture, 50 x 50 x 14 together; the artist's collection, photo Luke Unsworth © Aleksander Zyśko

9   Aleksander Zyśko, *Cross in Cross*, 1990, bronze sculpture, 53 x 35 x 19, the artist's collection, photo Luke Unsworth © Aleksander Zyśko

10   Harald Hauswald, *Time Travels*, 2008, photo installation (15 black-and-white photographs taken in various years), some gloss, some matt, each 37 x 33 (landscape form), the artist's collection, photo Jutta Vinzent and Antonia Grousdanidou © Harald Hauswald

11   Harald Hauswald, *Brandenburg Gate, Berlin 22 December 1989* (part of *Time Travels*, 2008), photo Antonia Grousdanidou

12   Harald Hauswald, *Brandenburg Gate, Berlin 1982* (part of *Time Travels*, 2008), photo Antonia Grousdanidou

13   Harald Hauswald, *Pariser Platz, Berlin 2005* (part of *Time Travels*, 2008), photo Antonia Grousdanidou

14   Harald Hauswald, *Brandenburg Gate, Berlin 2005* (part of *Time Travels*, 2008), photo Antonia Grousdanidou

15   Harald Hauswald, *Brandenburg Gate, Berlin 2000* (part of *Time Travels*, 2008), photo Antonia Grousdanidou

16   Harald Hauswald, *Brandenburg Gate, Berlin 2005* (part of *Time Travels*, 2008), photo Antonia Grousdanidou

17   Harald Hauswald, *Schlossplatz, Berlin 1982* (part of *Time Travels*, 2008), photo Antonia Grousdanidou

18   Harald Hauswald, *Procession of the Dukes, Dresden 1984* (part of *Time Travels*, 2008), photo Antonia Grousdanidou

19   Harald Hauswald, *Potsdamer Platz, Berlin 2005* (part of *Time Travels*, 2008), photo Antonia Grousdanidou

20   Harald Hauswald, *Alexanderplatz, Berlin 2006* (part of *Time Travels*, 2008; middle row), photo Antonia Grousdanidou

21   Harald Hauswald, *Alexanderplatz, Berlin 2006* (part of *Time Travels*, 2008; bottom row), photo Antonia Grousdanidou

22   Harald Hauswald, *Berlin 1 May 1987* (part of *Time Travels*, 2008), photo Antonia Grousdanidou

23   Harald Hauswald, *Berlin 1 May 1989* (part of *Time Travels*, 2008), photo Antonia Grousdanidou

24   Harald Hauswald, *Underground Line A, Berlin 1986* (part of *Time Travels*, 2008), photo Antonia Grousdanidou

25   Harald Hauswald, *Procession of the Dukes, Dresden 2005* (part of *Time Travels*, 2008), photo Antonia Grousdanidou

26   Sándor Pinczehelyi, *Almost 30 Years*, 1973-2002, silkscreen, 140 x 100 and 140 x 100 (140 x 200 together), the artist's collection, photo Luke Unsworth © Sándor Pinczehelyi

27   Sándor Pinczehely, *Star (Cobblestone)*, 1973, reproduced in *Art Eon. Magazyn o sztuce*, no. 4, 2007, 23 © Sándor Pinczehelyi

28   Ulf Göpfert, *Individuality Versus Dictatorship*, 2008, sculpture (mixed media), 1 x 0,5 x 0,6 m without the box, the artist's collection, photo Luke Unsworth © Ulf Göpfert

29   View into the barrel of Ulf Göpfert, *Individuality Versus Dictatorship*, 2008, photo Luke Unsworth

30   Zbyněk Benýšek, *Prague Buffet*, 1996, oil on canvas, 100 x 150, the artist's collection, photo Luke Unsworth © Zbyněk Benýšek

31   Aleksander Zyśko, *Obelisk*, 2007, installation (mixed media: iron frame, paint on canvas and sawdust), 285 x 80 x 80 (excluding the sawdust), the artist's collection, photo Luke Unsworth © Aleksander Zyśko

32   Detail of Aleksander Zyśko, *Obelisk*, 2007, photo Luke Unsworth

33 Silvestro Lodi, *Hanging History – Stock of History*,
    2007–2008, installation (mixed media: photography
    and oil on wood, cord, cardboard, hanger), 200 x 100,
    the artist's collection, photo Silvestro Lodi
    © Silvestro Lodi

34 Silvestro Lodi, *Hanging History – Stock of History*,
    2007–2008, schematic view of the work with the same
    title, photo Silvestro Lodi

35 Silvestro Lodi, *My Own Hanging History – My Stock
    of History*, 2008, installation (mixed media:
    photography and oil on wood, cord, cardboard,
    hanger), 200 x 102 cm, the artist's collection,
    photo Silvestro Lodi © Silvestro Lodi

36 Silvestro Lodi, *My Own Hanging History – My Stock
    of History*, 2008, schematic view of the work with the
    same title, photo Silvestro Lodi

37 Sándor Pinczehelyi, *XYZ*, 1973, reproduced in Lóránd
    Hegyi, Pinczehelyi, exh. cat., Pécs, 1995, 39
    © Sándor Pinczehelyi

38 Jens Rudolph, *Staats_Sicherheit*, 2004, film still,
    photo www.acc-weimar.de

39 Peggy Meinfelder, *My First 100,- Westmark*, installa-
    tion view, ACC Galerie, Weimar, 2004,
    photo www.acc-weimar.de

40 Mirela Dauceanu, *Daily Invalid Corruption*,
    1995/2008, installation (mixed media: recycled fridge
    and TV, medicine), 85 x 55 x 60, the artist's collection,
    photo Luke Unsworth © Mirela Dauceanu

41 Mirela Dauceanu, *Daily Invalid Corruption*, 1995,
    installation (mixed media: recycled fridge and TV,
    medicine), photo Mirela Dauceanu © Mirela Dauceanu

42 Clive Barber, *Fridge*, no date, installation (mixed
    media), 133 high, reproduced in Peter Blake (ed.),
    Royal Academy Illustrated 2001, Royal Academy of
    Arts, London 2001, 43

43 Detail of Mirela Dauceanu, *Daily Invalid Corruption*,
    1995, photo Mirela Dauceanu

44 Detail of Mirela Dauceanu, *Daily Invalid Corruption*,
    1995/2008, photo Luke Unsworth

45 Zbyněk Benýšek, *Midnight Watch*, 2007, oil on canvas,
    150 x 220, the artist's collection, photo Luke Unsworth
    © Zbyněk Benýšek

46 Michele Zaggia, *Unpredicted Outcome*, 2007, film
    (5 min. 10 sec.), the artist's collection, photo (cover)
    Jutta Vinzent © Michele Zaggia

47 Film still (00:08) from Michele Zaggia, *Unpredicted
    Outcome*, 2007, photo Barbara Lubich

48 Film still (01:23) from Michele Zaggia, *Unpredicted
    Outcome*, 2007, photo Barbara Lubich

49 Film still (00:44) from Michele Zaggia, *Unpredicted
    Outcome*, 2007, photo Barbara Lubich

50 Film still (01:33) from Michele Zaggia, *Unpredicted
    Outcome*, 2007, photo Barbara Lubich

51 Film still (02:01) from Michele Zaggia, *Unpredicted
    Outcome*, 2007, photo Barbara Lubich

52 Film still (03:57) from Michele Zaggia, *Unpredicted
    Outcome*, 2007, photo Barbara Lubich

53 Film still (04:04) from Michele Zaggia, *Unpredicted
    Outcome*, 2007, photo Barbara Lubich

54 Zbigniew Czop, *Together – Separately*, n.d., etching,
    29.7 x 42, the artist's collection, photo Zbigniew Czop
    © Zbigniew Czop

55 Vlad Nancă, *I Do Not Know What Union I Want to
    Belong to Anymore*, 2003, installation (mixed media:
    screen print on textile), 132 x 88 (each of the two flags
    without the poles), the artist's collection,
    photo Luke Unsworth © Vlad Nancă

56 Jan Nálevka, *We Will Meet Again*, installation view,
    Futura Gallery, Prague, 2006, photo Futura Gallery,
    Prague

57 Vlad Nancă, *Ideal*, 2007, installation (textile on flag
    poles), 135 x 90 (each of the three flags without the
    poles), the artist's collection, photo Luke Unsworth
    © Vlad Nancă

58 Flag of Romania between 1965 and 1989,
    photo Wikimedia Commons

59 Flag of the GDR between 1959 and 1990, photo
    Wikimedia Commons

60 Flag of Hungary between 1949 and 1956,
    photo Wikimedia Commons

61 Zbigniew Czop, *Awful Pedagogy*, 1986, etching,
    29.7 x 42, the artist's collection, photo Zbigniew Czop
    © Zbigniew Czop

Index

The Deutsche Bibliothek holds a record of this
publication in the Deutsche Nationalbibliografie; detailed
bibliographical data can be found under: www.dnb.ddb.de

Printed and published by
Kerber Verlag, Bielefeld
Windelsbleicher Straße 166-170
33659 Bielefeld
Germany
Tel. +49 5 21- 9 50 08-10
Fax +49 5 21- 9 50 08-88
email: info@kerberverlag.com
www.kerberverlag.com

Kerber, US Distribution
D.A.P., Distributed Art Publishers Inc.
155 Sixth Avenue 2nd Floor
New York, N.Y. 10013
Tel. +1 212 6 27-19 99
Fax +1 212 6 27-94 84

© 2008 Kerber Verlag, Bielefeld/Leipzig
Authors, Publisher and Artists

graphic design: jungundwenig

ISBN 978-3-86678-178-8

Printed in Germany

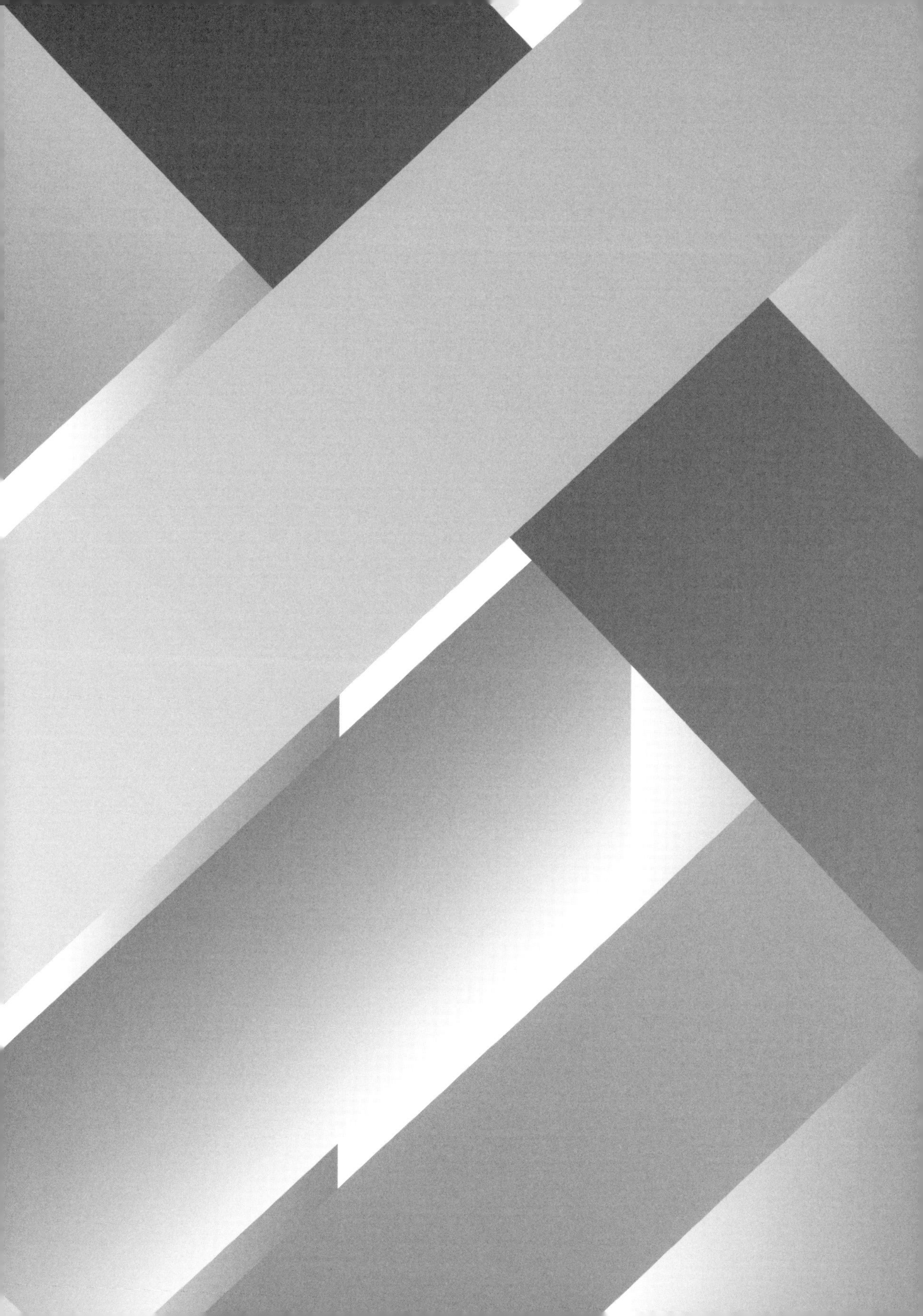

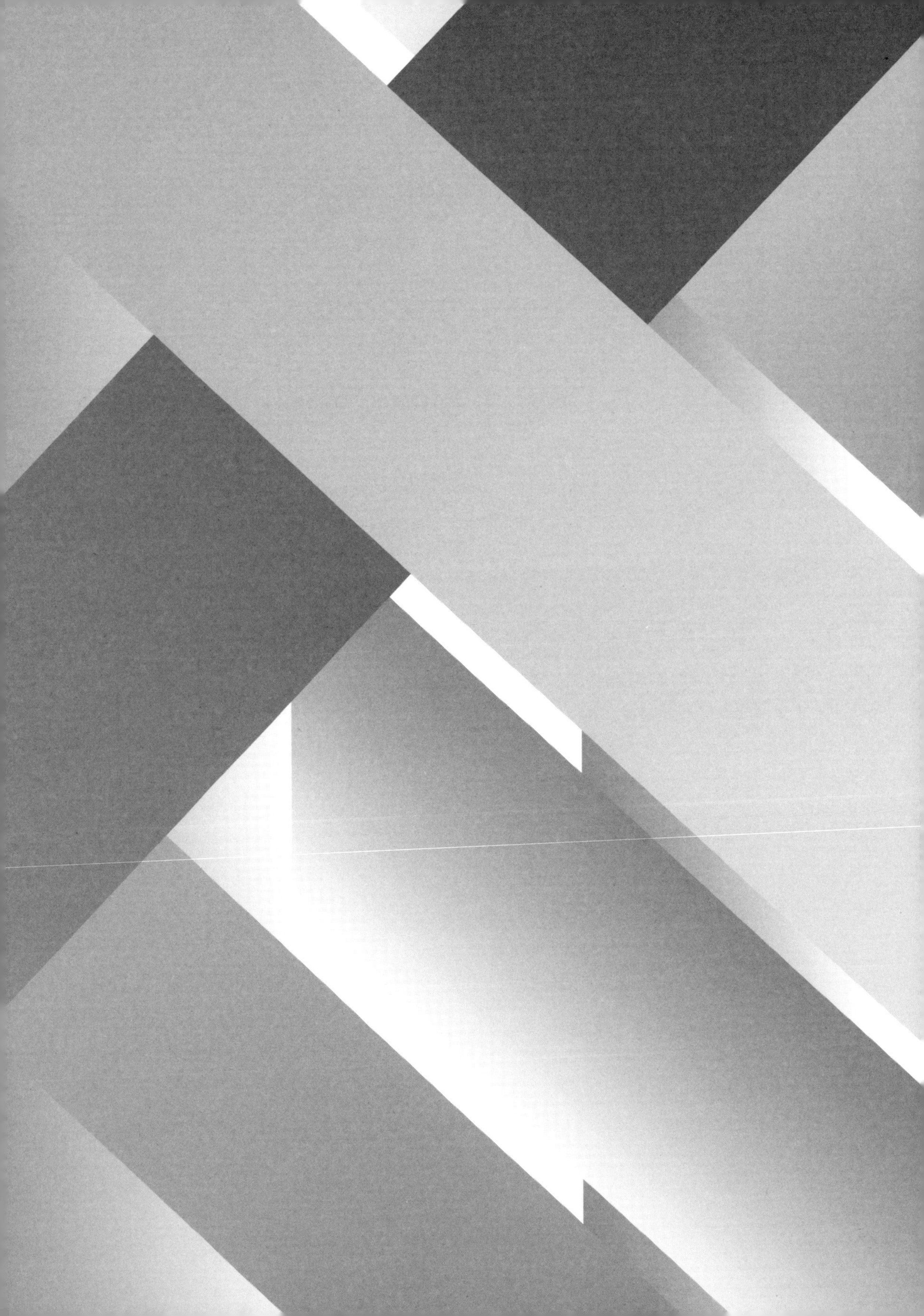